SEARCH ENGINE MARKETING FOR ECOMMERCE BUSINESSES

Copyright © 2019 Joe Balestrino

All rights reserved. No part of this publication may be reproduced, distributed, or transmitted in any form or by any means, including photocopying, recording, or other electronic or mechanical methods, without the prior written permission of the publisher, except in the case of brief quotations embodied in critical reviews and certain other noncommercial uses permitted by copyright law. For permission requests, write to the publisher below.

Joe@JoeBalestrino.com
https://JoeBalestrino.com

SEARCH ENGINE MARKETING

FOR ECOMMERCE BUSINESSES

JOE BALESTRINO

CONTENTS

About the Author: Joe Balestrino 1
Who Is This Book For? 3
First Impressions Count 5
The Importance of Product Pages 7
    Elements to Add to A Product Page 7
    What Are Trust Signals? 8
    Other "Signals" You Can Use on Product Pages 9
    Category Page Optimization 10
    Category Page Features 10
The Importance of Page Speed 12
    Image Optimization 14
    On-Page Optimization 14
    Ecommerce Site Structure 15
    Category Page Optimization 15
    Site Navigation 16
Products and Pricing 18
    The Importance of Inventory 18
    Price Your Products Competitively 19
    Keyword Research 20
    Category Page Optimization 20
    Why Use This Method Over A Keyword Tool? 23
How to Write Title Tags for Product Pages 24
    Meta Description Optimization for Ecommerce 25
    How to Name Products 26
    The Difference Between Product Titles and Title Tags ... 28
    Product Description Optimization 29
Ecommerce SEO Strategy 31
    How to Use Google Shopping 34
    How to Optimize Your Google Shopping Feed 34
Campaign Management 37

- Google Shopping Ads Troubleshooting 40
- Product Descriptions 40

Product Category 42
- GTIN – Global Item Number 43
- Reasons to use a GTIN 43
- Sales and Merchant Promotions 43
- Product Type 44
- Product Image Optimization 45
- Optimize the Google Merchant Center 46
- Regularly Update the Feed Data 48
- Analyze Ad Performance Data 48

How to Optimize Google Shopping Ads 49
- Automated Bidding for Google Shopping 49
- Rule-Based Bidding 50
- Optimize Product Images 51
- Add Negative Keywords 52
- Use Promotion Codes 53
- Breaking Out Products 54
- What Are Google Smart Shopping Ads? 57
- What Is Smart Bidding? 59
- Who Can Use Smart Shopping Campaigns? 59
- How to Set Up Smart Shopping Campaigns 60
- Best Practice for Smart Shopping Ads 61
- Pros of Google Smart Shopping 62
- Cons of Smart Shopping Campaigns 63
- Should You Use Smart Shopping Campaigns? 64
- Minimum Amount for Google Ads Campaign? 65

Ecommerce Blogging 67
- What will you learn from this section? 67
- What Should You Write About? 68
- How to Conduct Keyword Research? 69
- How Much Content Should You Write? 73
- What Type of Information Should Be Included in Your Content? 74

How to Structure Your Content 75
A Working Example 76
How to Turn Your Content into a Sales Tool 78
How to Optimize for Featured Snippets 81
Should You Write All the Content Yourself? 84
    On-Page Blog Optimization 85
What Title Tags Are Not 85
    What Is a Meta Description? 86
    What Are H1 Tags and How to Leverage Them? 86
How to Set Up Search Console & Google Analytics 89
How to Setup Google Analytics and Google Search
Console 92
    Submit Your Site to Google Search Console 92
    Google Analytics 93
    Google Tag Manager 94
    DNS 95
Linking Google Analytics With Google Search Console 96
    Choosing Analytics Property 96
    Choosing Search Console Property 97
    Linking Properties 99
How to Find Google Search Console Data in Google
Analytics 101
    Countries 102
    Devices Report 103
    Queries 103
How to Track Revenue and Leads in Google Analytics 104
    Identifying Goals 104
    How to Set Up Goals in Google Analytics 105
Create a New Goal 105
Choose Goal Setup 106
Goal Description 107

Fill in Goal Details 108
To Customize the Last Step 109
Start Recording 110
View Your Data 111
How to Set Up Google Analytics Ecommerce Tracking 112
Integrate Analytics with Google Ads 114
Integrated Analytics, Step by Step 114
Create Your SEO Dashboards 117
Monitoring Keywords 120
Tweaking and Optimizing Content 121
Why Traditional Link Building Isn't Always Necessary 124
What You Need to Build Links Naturally 124
Help Reporters Out and Gain a Link 126
Content That Speaks for Itself 127
The Right Way to Structure Your Blog 129
Why Not Just No, Index Tagged URLs? 130
How to Get More Out of The Content You Create 131
Existing Content Optimization 132

ABOUT THE AUTHOR
JOE BALESTRINO

Joe Balestrino started in digital marketing in 2004. He ran one of the fastest-growing digital agencies in New York. He built the business from the ground up and generated more than a quarter of a million dollars the first year with not a penny spent on advertising. Joe produced a ton of free content with the goal of educating website owners. He was one of the early pioneers of podcasting and had a very successful forum where business owners could come and discuss digital marketing.

Over the course of his career, Joe started his own SEO agency and sold it in 2008. He then began working in-house on the client-side as well as within other agencies. Joe trained entire editorial and marketing teams on both SEO and digital marketing as a whole. He's been interviewed by NBC, NPR radio, and quoted in many online and print publications as an expert in digital marketing.

Joe has spent many years learning, testing and perfecting his strategies when it comes to creating and growing SEO traffic for clients. Joe created this book for those small and mid-size businesses that are struggling to drive meaningful traffic to their website. Many business owners read about running an ecommerce business and blogging but don't know what that entails or how to be successful at both. There is also a lot of misinformation on the internet and it can be hard for a small business owner to understand how to structure an ecommerce site and how to drive traffic to it using content marketing.

While nothing is guaranteed when it comes to online marketing, there is one thing that will remain the same. As long as the internet exists and people use it to research, learn and shop, you can make money. You just need the right set of tools and accurate training.

WHO IS THIS BOOK FOR?

This book wasn't created to be a beginner's guide although beginners can use this book to gain more advanced knowledge of these marketing tactics. Ecommerce businesses have continued to grow year after year. There are over 500,000 active stores running on the Shopify platform alone, and they've collectively driven more than 40 billion dollars' worth of sales. It's easy to get swept up in all the hype.

Youtubers shout about all the millions they are making with dropshipping and ecommerce, however, these results aren't achievable for many people. These so-called gurus make it out to be a simple process that anyone can do. This is a ploy to get you to buy their course or membership. However, this type of "get rich" mentality isn't something someone can sustain for long.

I receive regular requests to audit ecommerce sites to review SEO, PPC, or both, for ecommerce owners. The majority of sites I review are all in very competitive spaces. They are typically clothing, home goods or electronics. Building a site in a competitive niche makes it very hard to compete with "big players", so I highly recommend that if you have not found your niche yet to try and find a niche that's not as competitive or find a smaller niche inside a larger one.

However, if you already have your niche and your site is built, no worries. This guide will help give you the edge you need to compete with the "big players", just on a different level. This is not an easy or fast process. If you think you can have a site up and running in a month, you won't. Attention to detail is required to be successful.

At the time of writing this book, I had created a Shopify store (https://thelavishminimalist.com/) to use as a real-time example that you can review as a study aid. I encourage you to check it out as you read through this book. I'll include images and screenshots in case the site is no longer available.

FIRST IMPRESSIONS COUNT

When all is said and done and you're getting good quality traffic to your site, it's your website's design that will be the deciding factor. If your site looks unprofessional, untrustworthy or the images look amateurish, you can kiss your sales good-bye.

Unfortunately, visitors judge a site's validity based on how a company's website looks. I've seen many long-standing companies who have been around for over 15 years that have a crummy website and drive very few sales, but a new company with a fresh clean look can outsell an outdated site easily. Most people *do not care* where they buy from, so long as the price is right, and the site appears to be legit.

The home page is usually the most viewed page of a site. It should convey a sense of high quality, which you can create with quality images. Your site should be clean and not cluttered. The current design of the homepage of my Shopify store is on the next page.

It pays to invest in a high-end look, especially if you want to sell more higher-end products. You're a business and you don't

want your site to look like it was built by an amateur. Review your competitor's websites and take note of the look and feel. Your site should be equal to or surpass them when it comes to design. If not, you'll spend more to generate sales.

What does this have to do with marketing? If you manage to get your site ranking on the first page of Google that doesn't guarantee sales. It's important that you understand what shoppers expect in their shopping experience; this will help your site sell more products.

THE IMPORTANCE OF PRODUCT PAGES

Your product pages need to load fast and have nice sharp images that showcase your products from different angles. You should always include important information and "signals" that will help visitors come to the decision to make a purchase.

Elements to Add to A Product Page

1. **Reviews** - Star reviews marked up with schema will show in search results, improving your CTR (Click Through Rate). It is also "social proof" that others have bought from you. This increases your ability to make a sale.

2. **CTA** - A clear call to action (CTA). Don't make it hard for a visitor to order your product or to find its cost.

3. **Trust signals** - When visitors aren't familiar with your brand or haven't ordered from you before, you want them to feel confident in their purchase.

What Are Trust Signals?

Trust signals are usually logos that give visitors a sense of trustworthiness. This could be something as simple as a secure shopping icon or a virus protection logo. These are logos that users trust, and therefore some of that trust is emulated on to your site. Here are a few good examples of how to leverage the items I mentioned above:

This site offers a clean professional look with a clear trust signal by indicating the number of reviews, a log displaying easy returns, free shipping and add to cart button that is all viewable at once. If the user never scrolls down the page (many never do), the company has provided a lot of important details buyers want to know.

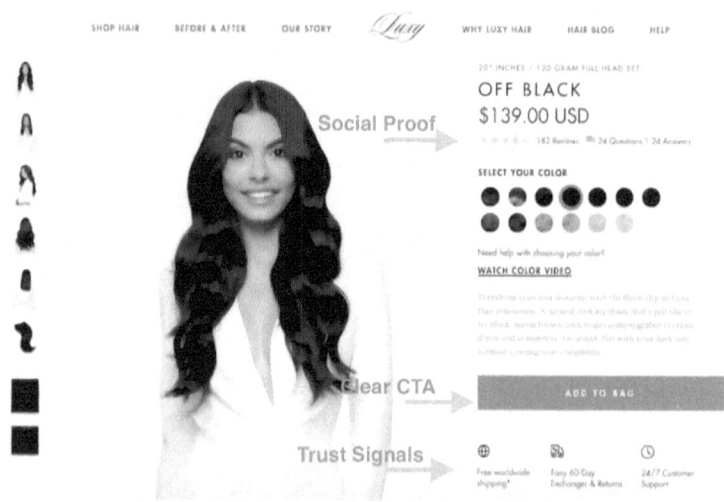

The product page below also has several elements that can help convert shoppers into buyers. There are reviews and a clear CTA button as well as trust signals, such as listing the number of overall reviews, awards, etc. located within the green box. Shoppers have the option of buying the product outright or paying monthly installments, as seen in the blue box. This is a great feature for all consumers to take advantage of, and it makes it easier for someone looking to buy this product to actually pull the trigger.

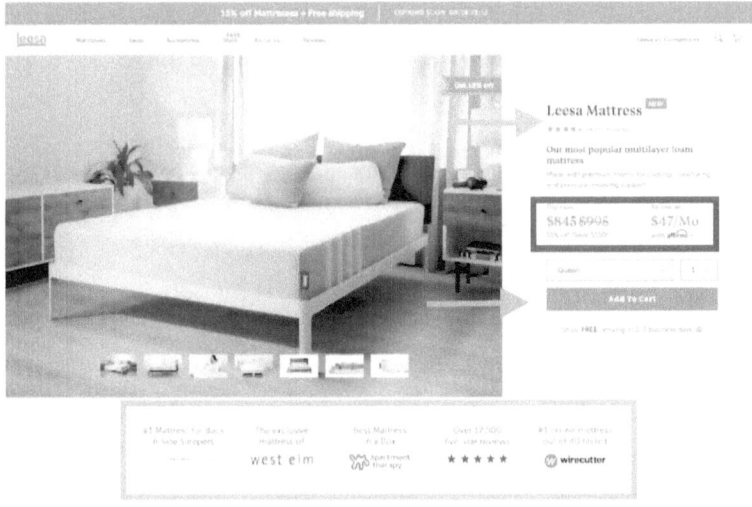

Other "Signals" You Can Use on Product Pages

- Guarantees
- BBB Rating
- Secure "ordering" logos
- Payment logos (Visa, Mastercard, AMEX, etc.)

Experiment with adding different trust logos to your product and checkout pages to see if they increase conversions.

It's a proven fact that reviews help with conversions. If you have a new site and don't have many reviews, it can be hard to get users to buy without them. If you are selling products sold by a manufacturer you may be able to use the reviews on their site (with permission). If you import products from AliExpress and use Shopify as your platform, there are plugins that can pull in reviews for you automatically. The upside to the plugins is that they will save you a lot of time getting reviews into your products however, take the time to read the reviews you import to make sure that the reviews are in English and make sense. Otherwise, they may do more harm than good.

Category Page Optimization

Category pages have a dual purpose. They can drive organic (SEO) traffic on slightly broader key terms and can also play a key role in your paid strategy if these pages are built out properly. The goal is to help users find what they want in as few clicks as possible. One way to do that is by constructing your category page for success.

Category Page Features

If I can target searchers (from paid ads) that are looking for something a little more specific, such as brown or black wallets, I could show them just that one color on a page. Making it easier to find something they like. If it isn't possible to send the customer directly to a "filtered" page, then have filters on categories that will allow visitors to sort and find what they are looking for. This could be by color, size, material, etc.

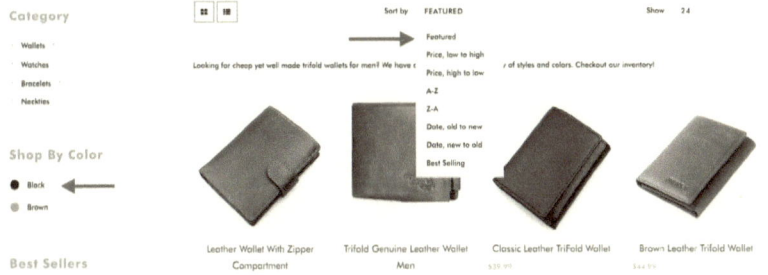

If you mouse over any wallet on my page, you will see what the inside of each wallet looks like. This allows visitors to view the inside of the product from a category perspective without clicking into the product, offering in my opinion, a better shopping experience.

Some clothing retailers show the details of their products. What you decide to do is entirely up to you. You should review your site as a customer, not a business owner. Ask friends and relatives to give you their opinion on the site. Know what your customers want to see, what information they need to know and give it to them so that they can buy!

It's important to take time to design a good user experience. Paying for traffic and ranking for phrases means little if you can't convert searchers into buyers.

THE IMPORTANCE OF PAGE SPEED

It's not a myth. If your webpages are slow to load, you'll not only lose search engine ranking, but you will also limit the amount of traffic you will receive from Google. User experiences will be poor for anyone, regardless of how they find your site. This will cause visitors to leave before your content even loads.

Google offers a free site speed testing tool. This tool will crawl your web page (not the entire site) and identify what may be causing your site to slow down.

Opportunity	Estimated Savings
▲ Serve images in next-gen formats	6.45 s
▲ Defer offscreen images	4.2 s
▲ Efficiently encode images	4.2 s
▲ Eliminate render-blocking resources	3.24 s
▲ Avoid multiple page redirects	1.74 s
▬ Enable text compression	0.45 s
▬ Properly size images	0.3 s
▬ Minify JavaScript	0.15 s
▬ Remove unused CSS	0.15 s

Some Common Resources That Can Slow Load Times:

- Not utilizing web caching
- Large CSS and JavaScript's
- Large or uncompressed images
- Not removing WordPress plugins that aren't being used

If you're using WordPress, there are many free and paid plugins that you can use to help improve the speed of your site.

WP Rocket Includes ($49):

- Page caching
- Cache pre-load
- CDN integration
- Image lazy loading
- User-friendly interface
- Database optimization
- Advanced caching rules
- Minify CSS, HTML and JavaScript

WP Fastest Cache Includes (Free):

- Easy setup
- CDN integration
- Minify CSS and HTML
- 1-click to clear cache and/or minified CSS

There are plenty of plugins to choose from. However, it's better to get an all-in-one plugin that can handle multiple aspects of improving your site's overall speed versus downloading several separate plugins. As you add them, they can input more code to your site, slowing down performance.

Image Optimization

Ecommerce sites tend to have a lot of images. The more images that are on a page the longer it can take for the page to load.

If you sell a product with multiple images, it can really impact load time. In my work with site owners, I have often seen them mistakenly assume that uploading and resizing an image to make it smaller will speed up the page's load time. The site builder auto-shrinks the image size. However, the platform you are on doesn't compress the image for faster loading. You will need to do that before you upload the image.

You could grab an app on Shopify or WordPress that will compress your images, enabling them to load faster. If you're feeling lazy, you can purchase ShortPixel for WordPress and it will resize and optimize your images. If you don't have WordPress, you can still use the tool to resize and compress by uploading your images to the site.

On-Page Optimization

On-page optimization is the foundation of your ecommerce site. If your on-page optimization isn't on point, it won't matter how many links you have directing people to your site, as anything else you do will not help. This process is not complicated, but it is time-consuming. You will need to repeat this process every time you add a new product. Don't take shortcuts; avoid copying and pasting product and title info straight from the manufacturer. This will decrease your chances of driving organic traffic.

Ecommerce Site Structure

Before launching your site, it's important to plan your site's architecture and keyword usage to improve your ecommerce SEO. This book will help you build a solid foundation that many ecommerce sites lack. The majority of effort is usually placed on the choice of products and the design of the site. Many sites fall short in not taking the time and effort to make their site and content different than every other site.

In the eyes of Google, it's okay to sell the same products. What is not okay is to use the same descriptions and titles for those products. Think about the experience. How boring would the internet be? Being different is what makes the internet interesting. This will play a major role in the success of your site.

Category Page Optimization

There should be a clear structure for your site. In this example, I have "men's watches" broken down by different watch styles. Why is this important? Why not just place all of the watches in one category? The goal is to get as detailed as possible for a few reasons.

People generally search by type; no one searches for just "watches," as it's too broad. People tend to have a style of watch that they want to buy. If someone was looking for a "men's minimalist watch" style, they may search "minimalist watches for men" or "men's minimalist watches."

You might be thinking that the term is too broad or too competitive, which is a valid concern. However, for me, this is a longer-term SEO goal. I want to break these watches into as many tightly grouped product categories as possible, not just for SEO.

If I wanted to send visitors from paid search campaigns to my site, I could bid on terms around "minimalist watches" and send them to this landing page, which only features this one style. This improves quality score and performance.

It pays to do your research and see how many categories you can create with your products. It doesn't matter if products fall into multiple categories. The duplicate content will be minimal as long as all of the same products don't appear in every single category in the same way.

Site Navigation

Google places more value on links that are found on every page, either through a main or sub-navigation. This is a signal to Google that these pages are important because you've made them accessible from every page of the site. You should group products together as logically as possible.

As you can see, I've grouped my "men's wallet" navigation together by the type of wallet and by type of material.

I could get even more detailed if I wanted to. I could have broken "trifold wallets" into a sub-navigation for "trifold leather wallets." However, I didn't have enough wallets to fill that category.

PRO TIP: Links found in the footer have less value than those found in the main navigation bar. Google knows few people scroll to the bottom of the page. Usually links such as "contact us," "privacy policy" and "social media" are found in the footer. Therefore, it's important to place all of your important links in the main navigation bar. Alternatively, do not place "contact us," "FAQs," or any social media links or other non-money pages in the header. Save that prime real estate for important money-generating pages.

PRODUCTS AND PRICING

While this isn't necessarily search marketing, it is important to understand how a product's price, as well as the overall number of site products, can have on your site and influence your sales. Do not overlook this part of the process. Knowing what your competitors are charging is one of the key factors to outperform them.

The Importance of Inventory

When creating category and subcategory pages, you need to take into account the number of products that are in each category. Even though we are grouping products specifically, if there are not enough products for shoppers to choose from, they will shop elsewhere. I recommend having at least 12 products or more in a category or subcategory.

If there aren't enough products on a site when a customer browses, it may come across as the site not being "legitimate." The site will look bare and unappealing. Before you start spending money on advertising your site, be sure you have enough products to fill out your category pages. If you only have 24 products in one category, make your category pages show only 8-10 products per page. This will create 3-4 pages of products for people to browse.

Price Your Products Competitively

Pricing plays a big role in converting browsers into buyers. As I stated earlier, "most people *do not care* where they buy from so long as the price is right and the site appears to be legit." Your pricing needs to be on par with your competitors. If your product cost is higher, you need to justify that quickly. Otherwise, the visitor will find it elsewhere for cheaper.

A more high-end web design doesn't mean you can charge more if everyone else is charging less. If your prices are the same as those of your competitors, how will you convince them to buy from you instead? What do you offer that they don't?

- Free shipping?
- Express shipping?
- Next day shipping?
- Gift opportunities?

Review your competitors' sites and see how you can entice people to buy from you instead of them.

I once had a site that sold sunglasses. I offered visitors a free eyeglass cleaning spray and cloth with each order of over $50. The kit cost me .60. That offer increased my sales by 27 percent. Think about what you can offer to swing the odds in your favor.

Keyword Research

This section is going to be for your category pages. As described earlier, the first step is to group your products into categories. You may not build them all out, but the more detailed you can get, the easier it will be for you to visualize your site structure and plan for future growth.

Category Page Optimization

Let's say there is a clothing shop that sells blouses for women. That would be the main category. How can we break this category out further?

- Style
- Color
- Brand
- Patterns
- Long sleeve
- Short sleeve

How many long sleeve blouses do you have? Enough to create a category? What about short sleeve blouses? Do you sell any well-known brands? Do you sell various striped blouses?

If you sell long, short, a brand name, and striped blouses, you could create a category for each. This is useful for two reasons. If someone is looking for a "short sleeve women's blouses"- searchers will ideally land on this page. We know searchers want a short sleeve blouse, but we don't know what color or style. All of our short sleeve blouses go here.

Now, if we sold a particular "brand" of short sleeve blouse, we could create a category for that, and the term could be brand + short sleeve + blouse or short + sleeve + blouses + brand". You could use the keyword research method described in this book to discover if people are searching that way. If you have enough of a selection it would be worth creating a section for it. However, if you don't you could just create a section for the brand and blouses.

If you only sold "plus-size" blouses, then your title tag would include "plus-size". Leaving that phrase out of the title tag of your category would cause you to miss out on a ton of organic traffic. Let's take a look at how people are searching.

Our category blouse section could read, "plus-size blouses on sale." That's a nice, long-tail phrase, which is exactly what we sell. I would stay away from terms such as "summer" as we want traffic all year round unless of course, this was keyword research for a blog post. Then you could create a post on "the most popular blouses for summer."

We then need to add a small amount of content to help Google understand a bit more about this section. Writing

Plus size blouses

plus size blouses
plus size blouses **on sale**
plus size blouses **walmart**
plus size blouses **for work**
plus size blouses **with collars**
plus size blouses **near me**
plus size blouses **and tops**
plus size blouses **for summer**
plus size blouses **cheap**
plus size blouses **macys**

just a few sentences reinforcing what is in the title tag will go a long way. This content should go above the list of products, not below. The description could read, "Check out our wide selection of plus-size blouses on sale in a variety of styles and colors. We offer free shipping on orders over $50 and a 30-day hassle-free return policy."

You could also mention other types of blouses that you sell and link to those in the description. This is not only good for SEO, but it is beneficial for users looking for something more specific. I would recommend not adding more than four sentences before the products. If you feel you need or want to add more, you can then add the rest of the content below the products. If you have too much content, people may not see any products when the page loads and leave your site.

In my example site, I sell watches, wallets, and ties for men. Let's take a look at one of my main categories, "minimalist wallets." I'll drop this phrase into Google and see the recommended searches are shown to me.

I can see that minimalist "watches for men" shows as a recommendation. That's exactly what I offer. If I wanted to, I could create another page for minimalist watches under $50 (which I did) or those closer to $500.

Google minimalist watches
minimalist watches **women**
minimalist watches **for men**
minimalist watches **reddit**
minimalist watches **under 100**
minimalist watches **under 50**
minimalist watches **brands**
minimalist watches **amazon**
minimalist watches **automatic**
minimalist watches **under 200**
minimalist watches **wholesale**

Why Use This Method Over A Keyword Tool?

You could pay for a keyword research tool. However, the data within these tools are estimates and are often inaccurate. If you use Google's free keyword tool within Google Ads, the data is also skewed, making it hard to gather accurate analytics. As a new site, you don't have the trust and authority to rank for one, two or even three competitive keywords or phrases. Most likely, the terms you want to go after won't have any data from these tools.

PRO TIP: Filters play an important role in helping users find products quickly. It can also help with your paid search campaigns. If I wanted to create a paid Google Ad campaign (non-shopping) to all short sleeve red blouses, I could adjust my filters to create those URLs, if I didn't have pages build for them already. You should verify that the filtered URL can be viewed by others and not just by you. Open the URL in an incognito browser to see if the filter page loads. This is a great way to get sales at a lower cost per conversion.

HOW TO WRITE TITLE TAGS FOR PRODUCT PAGES

Title tags for ecommerce sites can be tricky, especially when you sell many of the same product. The site I am using is fairly new and while "minimalist watches for men" is a long-tail term and should be easier to rank, I decided to go with "cheap minimalist watches for men." The competition is less and it tacks on another word to my phrase. The ultimate goal is to rank for variations of "cheap minimalist watches for men," "minimalist watches for men," and "cheap minimalist watches."

I also added a small blurb above the watches category page to add the term "cheap" to my other keywords for that section. I wanted to have those phrases found on the page in addition to the title.

As you can see, it appears to be doing well. There are various terms that the page ranks for and while there aren't a lot of monthly searches for these terms, (we know this information is not accurate anyway,) it's exactly in line with what the page sells and should resonate well with searchers.

Meta Description Optimization for Ecommerce

Meta descriptions are seen in Google search results. It tells searchers what they can find on the page, providing a great opportunity to entice searchers to click and visit your site. Clicks and time spent on your site improve your Google ranking. This shows that users are finding your site relevant and useful.

Here is an example of what a bad meta description looks like:

> Imperial Crown And Helmet Charm Bracelet For Men – The Lavish ...
> https://thelavishminimalist.com/collections/all/.../imperial-crown-helmet-charm-bracele... ▼
> ★★★★★ Rating: 4.8 - 8 reviews
> Brand Name: NAIQUBEBracelets Type: Charm BraceletsMetals Type: CopperGender: UnisexClasp Type: Hidden-safety-claspStyle: TrendyMaterial: ...

The meta description above will not receive many clicks, as there is no description. In many cases, searchers will skip this page altogether, even though it has reviews. Here is a better description that could encourage someone to check out the product:

> **Bluetooth Wallet Tracker For Men – The Lavish Minimalist**
> https://thelavishminimalist.com/collections/all/products/leather-bluetooth-wallet ▼
> ★★★★★ Rating: 4.8 - 11 reviews
> Never lose your wallet again. This new advanced Bluetooth wallet will remind you when you've left it behind. You can grab the traditional size or a more vertical ...

As you can see, there is a difference between the two. Never leave your meta description blank. This also pertains to category pages as well. You should write a description that gets users to check out your products.

How to Name Products

After you create your category page, it's time to work on naming your products. Here is where *83 percent* of ecommerce stores fail! If you are using the same product titles as the manufacturer, you'll run into a few issues:

Duplicated content – Google doesn't want to show the same exact product title in its search results. That would be a boring experience for users, so these are filtered out.

Long titles - Many product titles, especially from manufacturers such as AliExpress, are long, wordy and spammy. They will make your product titles unappealing to visitors and will clutter your website. You also won't drive any organic traffic with keyword-stuffed title tags.

If you don't create unique content in these areas, you will be missing out on driving organic traffic to your product pages.

I'll use my "minimalist watches" as an example. Take a look at these titles and tell me if you can spot what it is that I am doing.

Simple Mens Watch With Date   Mesh Band Minimalist Watch   Mens Quartz Mesh Band Watch   Casual Mens Watch With Mesh Band

The goal here is to use descriptive keywords to describe each watch in an attempt to get specific traffic to the product page. These watches are not made by well-known brands, so I am not using the name in the title tag or the product naming. When naming products, think of words that you would use to describe what the item looks like.

I use words that describe the product such as; mesh bands, casual, quartz, and minimalist. I never use the same keywords in the same order, and I try to point out the uniqueness of each watch. As an example, my "numberless watch" is one of my most organically-sold watches because I used "minimalist" and "numberless" in the title and it ranks for various terms. Since it resonates with searchers, they tend to buy it.

When people know what they want, they will type those descriptive terms into the search bar. A "white long sleeve blouse with red butterflies" is very specific, which you are more likely to rank for and convert on than just "white blouses." Just because a term is "long-tailed," doesn't mean it won't drive traffic or sales.

The Difference Between Product Titles and Title Tags

As you've already learned, title tags show up in search results and in your browser tab. However, the product title is what shows on the product and category page. These do not have to be the same and frankly, they shouldn't. There are two reasons why you would want these to be different.

If your "on page" product names are long, wordy and have keywords that don't make sense, the product pages will look messy.

If I wanted to use the word "cheap," I would want that term to be in the title tag and not in the product title itself.

Here is a good example of how to label items. Notice how each dress title is a description of what the dresses actually are.

While this is a bit wordy, none of these titles are longer than the other, keeping the uniformity of the site. This site uses the same title format throughout and in the title tag. You could keep these as title tags, or shorten the on-page product titles. I also might have capitalized the first letter of each word, but that's just me.

Product Description Optimization

Here is another place where ecommerce shops often fail. If you are using the same product description as the manufacturer, you are going to miss out on organic traffic. Your product descriptions need to be unique. The goal is to have the main keywords that you're going after in the description. If this is my title...

> Stainless Steel Mesh Watch In Multiple Colors - The Lavish ...
> ★★★★★ Rating: 5 - 8 reviews
> **Stainless steel** and **mesh** team up to create an industrialized **watch**. Simple, yet functional in design, the shiny **watch** is just what you need to keep punctual and ...

My product description would mention these words:

Stainless steel and mesh team up to create an industrialized watch. Simple yet functional in design, this shiny watch is just what you need to keep yourself punctual and on track. Designed for business or pleasure, the timepiece is lightweight and easy to wear. Choose from tones ranging from black to gold to rose gold, or even silver, all of which will enhance your business and casual wardrobes.

I also want all the sizes and colors that I carry in the product description to help with SEO and Google Shopping. I may sell a minimalist watch with a mesh band that comes in gold, silver, and red. I'll add that to my description while leaving the colors out of the title tag. I also want the description to talk about the material. Remember, you want someone to buy the product, so give them the information they need to make a purchase.

Is this time-consuming? Yes! It takes time to come up with unique descriptions. You can hire people to write the descriptions for you on websites such as Upwork. It typically costs 1-3 dollars per description. To start, you can get by with 3-5 lines for a description to start out with. You can use the same product dimensions as the manufacturer, but not the same description. Never post a product without a description. Make sure to include size, weight and any necessary dimensions as it pertains to your product.

ECOMMERCE SEO STRATEGY

In my experience, I have worked on a large range of ecommerce websites. Unless you have a lot of authority to help you rank for competitive keywords, this method will work best for you. Regardless of whether you use Shopify, WordPress or any other platform, the strategy for your ecommerce store should be as follows:

- Your Long-Term Strategy - To build SEO for category pages on broader terms, but also on specific types, styles and brands of products.

- Your Short-Term Strategy - To go after descriptive keywords on product pages, as those will be easier to ran.

- Create blog posts that answer questions about your products, the issues/questions they solve and link and/or add products within those posts.

Let's go back to the terms I was optimizing my site for. Here is a ranking report of the keywords that I am tracking around the phrase "cheap minimalist watches." As you can see, I'm ranking fairly well, even though watch-related terms are fairly competitive.

You're probably thinking that I have a ton of links pointing to my store, right? Wrong! My domain authority is 5! To be completely transparent, many of the other terms I am going after don't rank at all. I also haven't done any re-optimization or link-building in the last six months. I also haven't started any blog writing to help drive additional traffic.

Below is data from the last 6 months of clicks from Google, which came from an inside search console.

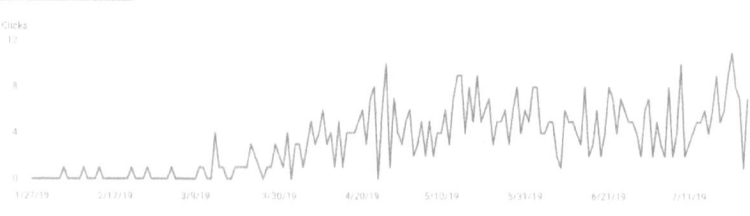

What can we learn from this data? It is possible to get organic traffic from Google, even if we are a new business? It comes down to long-tail terms and unique content. Here is the traffic over the last five months from Google Analytics. Again, I have not updated the site since it launched. I also have not added any new products, done any link building or tweaked any of my pages.

Source / Medium	Acquisition			Behavior			Conversions eCommerce		
	Users	New Users	Sessions	Bounce Rate	Pages / Session	Avg. Session Duration	Ecommerce Conversion Rate	Transactions	Revenue
	1,339	1,334	1,495	70.77%	1.87	00:01:10	0.40%	6	$213.89
1. google / organic	1,003	1,000	1,118	69.32%	1.92	00:01:07	0.36%	4	$154.91
2. (direct) / (none)	184	183	198	80.30%	1.51	00:00:41	1.01%	2	$58.98

As you can see, traffic is decent and there were a few orders. The conversions are low, as a good rate is about 3 percent. Still, a long way to go, but this is a good use case. Tracking your keywords and page performance will help improve rankings and performance. Tweak content, test different upsells, add social proof, use of pop-ups and other marketing tactics to improve the conversion rate of each page of your site.

PRO TIP: Domain authority is created by a company called Moz. You can download their extension to your browser. It ranks sites from 0-100 based on the tool's ability to identify the strength of backlinks pointing to your site. The higher the number, the stronger the DA of your site. You can use it to compare your site to others in your industry.

How to Use Google Shopping

Google shopping is one of the most effective ways to drive traffic to your ecommerce store. However, many website owners understand little about how to effectively set up and manage their shopping campaigns. This results in high costs with little results, causing many creators to determine that shopping campaigns aren't a valid source of sales. In this chapter, I'll explain more about shopping feeds and the different ways to use shopping ads to generate revenue.

How to Optimize Your Google Shopping Feed

The Google shopping feed is a spreadsheet that you provide to Google's Merchant Center that includes a description and categorization of your product catalog, provided in a way that Google can crawl and understand. Shopping campaigns work similarly to conventional search campaigns; instead of bidding on keywords, your ads will appear based on the optimization of your feed. You can also use services such as GoDataFeed that will build a feed for you, and certain platforms such as Shopify have plugins that do all the work for you.

The feed usually contains information such as brand name, availability and price, among other data points. Google Shopping will use the data to determine relevance, similar to how it is done with keywords in SEO. It is important to optimize your Google shopping feed; the more your ads show up in search results, the better the chance you have of a sale.

Product Titles

When you are optimizing your feed, the product title is the most important component. While you can send a lot of data to Google through your feed, product titles contribute up to 80 percent of your advertisement ranking on the search engines.

Google Shopping relies on the key terms in your product titles to understand how to identify and categorize the products. Nonetheless, product titles still need to have a natural structure that takes into account the needs of the consumer. The following are some of the most important elements to consider when optimizing your titles:

- **Character Limit** – Google allows you to input a maximum of 150 characters, though it is always recommended to input no more than 70 characters. If you go past 70 characters, Google will often truncate the titles.

- **Front Load Key Terms** – Put all your important and profitable keywords as close to the 70-character limit as possible.

Most Active Turmeric...
$39.95
Smarter Curcum
★★★★ (272)

Omega 3 Fish Oil Triple...
$49.99
Bronson Vitamin
Free shipping

Triple Strength Omega-3 Fish...
$22.38
Nutrigold.com
21% price drop

Sports Research,...
$35.95
iHerb
Free shipping

OmegaXL Powerful...
$39.95
OmegaXL

Puori O3 Fish Oil - Unflavore...
$37.00
The Feed
Free shipping

I searched for "OMEGA 3 fish oil." As you can see by the screenshot above, some of the products mention OMEGA 3, *or* fish oil. The products in red do not include any of the two words, though hovering over the ad shows that they do include it, meaning that it was truncated. Some of the bottles contain those keywords, and while helpful, they can be easily overlooked by the searcher.

Most people, especially those on mobile, will either not be able to, or will not bother to, hover over the ad, causing you to lose a lot of clicks by not frontloading your valuable keywords.

CAMPAIGN MANAGEMENT

In this chapter we cover how to optimize your Google shopping campaign, what to look at and what to change to get the most performance out of your account. When it comes to your product feed it is important to keep in mind the following.

Be Descriptive but Concise with Descriptions - You obviously have to include the name of the product you are selling, but make sure the description is something that both shoppers and the search engines need and want. For instance, accessories and apparel may include valuable information such as gender preference, size, and color. In certain verticals such as machines or auto parts manufacturers, numbers may be important to include as well.

Focus on Key Product Features - It is critical to remember that not all keywords have the same value. An important description in one keyword may not be as relevant for a different product. For example, model numbers are critical for electronics, but they often mean very little when it comes to apparel. It's important to check the ads of other advertisers.

Add Negative Keywords - Google will try and show your products for as many terms as possible. There will either be terms that are not relevant and need to be excluded or terms that are relevant and don't convert. You should go through the search term report and look at all of the keywords that are irrelevant or don't convert and exclude them. If you are using Google smart campaigns, you won't be able to see these terms in your account.

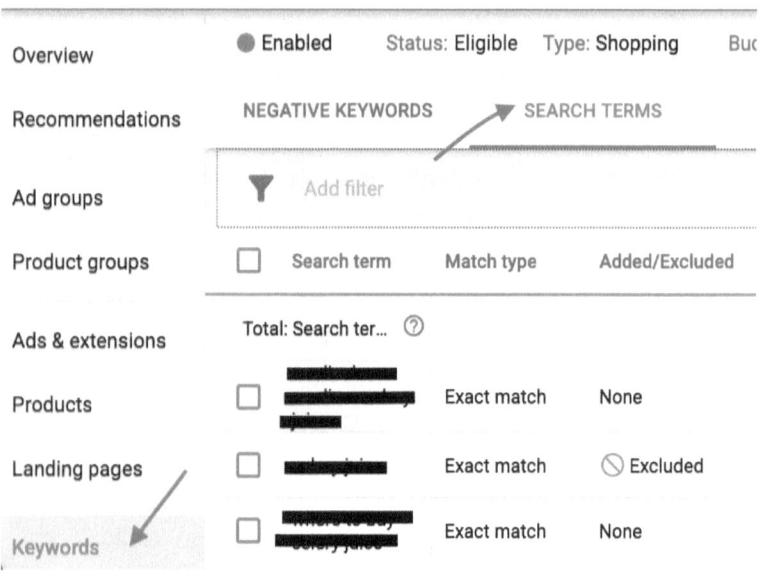

Pause Underperforming Products - If you've broken out your products inside Google Ads, you'll be able to view all of your products individually. Review them and go through those that have a poor conversion rate or a low ROAS. I try and shoot for a three-time ROI. Unless it's producing a lot of sales, anything under three should be paused.

If you have tracking sales value, adding Conv. value/cost will display how much you are spending versus what you are generating in revenue (you need to edit the code snippet to do so.)

☑ Conversions	☐ Cost / conv.	☐ Conv. rate	☐ Conv. value
☑ Conv. value / cost	☐ Conv. value / click	☐ Value / conv.	

It will look like this in your dashboard: A 3.0+ "All conv.value / cost" or more is a good ROI. The first row is making money but at less than 3 times it's spending budget. The second and third rows are making much more money than they are spending. You can improve these numbers by managing the campaign properly.

Cost	Conversion ↓	All conv. value	All conv. value / cost
$3,774.59	49.00	8,736.80	2.31
$107.58	38.00	7,951.08	73.91
$14.77	2.00	2,780.87	188.27

Increase Product Bids - As you review your account, make sure to look at the number of impressions each product is getting. If you see that certain products have low to no impressions, you should increase the bids. Keep doing so until you start getting views on those products. Over time, if increasing bids doesn't improve your position, try some of the below troubleshooting tips.

Google Shopping Ads Troubleshooting

When troubleshooting your ads, ask yourself the following questions:

- Do my Product Listing Ads appear when I run a manual search for product titles?
- Do my product descriptions or titles use the right keyword(s)?
- When I run a manual search, am I showing up for at least one product?

Product Descriptions

You can enter up to 5,000 characters for your product descriptions, though no shopper is likely to read that much information. In fact, having product descriptions that are too long may actually be negative for your product ads, since it could mean that you have unclear selling points and thus resulting in poor click-through rates. It can also result in your products showing up for a lot of irrelevant terms.

The optimal product description length is about 500 characters, no more than 1,000. To ensure that your descriptions are more effective, thoroughly research and use good keywords, just like you would when writing your meta descriptions and SEO titles.

PRO TIP: In the description of your product, don't compare your product to a competitor. Google may use those keywords to show your ad. If you compare your $20 watch to a Rolex, you may start showing up for Rolex watches, which would be a waste of money.

PRODUCT CATEGORY

The product category is algorithm-centric, rather than a consumer-facing metric. It's important to choose the right category as Google will use it when ranking your ad on its search results.

You need to include the product category in every shopping feed you submit, or the product ads will not be listed. Google provides the Google Product Taxonomy, also known as GPT, which is a list of more than 6,000 categories and subcategories that you can use to classify your product ads. You can find the complete list of them here on Google, or just by Googling "Google Product Taxonomy".

The product category is a critical component for optimizing your feed as it gives the ad relevance. The more accurate you are with your categories and subcategories, the more relevant the ad will be. This will result in more targeted clicks and better conversions.

GTIN - Global Item Number

If you are reselling goods provided by a manufacturer, the Global Trade Item is an important and mandatory component of optimization. However, if you are selling antiques and custom products/manufacturer parts are the only seller, you do not have to include the GTIN.

Reasons to use a GTIN

Google makes use of the GTIN in order to get the data from the supplier catalog. It then differentiates your products from those of other sellers that are reselling the same product. Most of the time, Google Shopping will override optimizations in the feed and use the attributes provided by the supplier.

GTINS can get your ad placed when searches such as "top" and "best" are included with certain keywords. Since these searches make use of customer reviews to rank ads, you stand a chance of ranking in the first position if the product is reviewed on sites such as Verified Reviews, Yotpo or Trustpilot.

Sales and Merchant Promotions

Merchant and sales promotions are among the best ways to drive high click-through rates and conversions at relatively lower costs. For instance, if you own an ecommerce store selling clothing and you are running a promotion at 30 percent off for the spring collection, you can set up a promotional code of SAVE30 on the site and include this in the shopping feed.

The first thing to do is to set up a promotion ID as an attribute and then populate all the clothing you intend to sell using the code. After logging into Google Merchant Center Account, you can select the promotions tab to create a promotion. Google Merchant Center will provide instructions on all-things promotions, including how to set them up, provide start and end dates, promotion codes, product specifications and more.

Merchant promotions and sales may run for up to four months without any updates. This can be great if you are running a long sale or if you are offering free shipping. They can include promotions such as:

- Free shipping

- Brand-specific rebates (sponsored by the manufacturer, one for each brand for example)

- Lowering free shipping thresholds

- Tiered percentage discounts, such as 20 percent off orders of $150 or more, 10 percent off on orders of $50

- Buy one, get one at 50 percent off or buy one, get one free

Product Type

The product type optimization is another important component that will help Google's backend determine relevance. Unlike the product category, this is not mandatory, but providing the type for your product ads can make for a more precise categorization of the ad, improving click-through rates and conversions. It allows the ecommerce seller to paint the product better, thus serving it to more relevant audiences. Product type may be especially important for ecommerce sellers that sell niche products that are unlikely to be featured on the GPT.

Product Image Optimization

Product images are important for your product ads in Google Shopping. It is worth investing in images as they will pay for themselves in better click-through rates and conversions.

Follow these guidelines to optimize your images in Google Shopping:

- Include at least three good quality images for every product.

- Ensure the image is on a white background and provides a clear view of the product.

- Images should not have any watermarks or text of any kind. This includes:

    - Calls to action, for example, "buy"
    - Service-related information such as extended warranty
    - Free shipping
    - Price information
    - Promotional adjectives–for example, "best," or "cheap"
    - Condition or compatibility–for example, "new," "2-piece," or "adaptable"
    - Any overlay–for example, watermarks, brand names or logos

- Barcodes
- Brand / manufacturer / retailer name or logo

• If you are selling accessories, clothing or shoes, provide images showing different angles.

• Avoid using placeholder images or images with a dark background.

• Have images with the best resolution you can find:
    - Non-apparel images: at least 100 x 100 pixels
    - Apparel images: at least 250 x 250 pixels
    - No image larger than 64 megapixels
    - No image file larger than 16MB

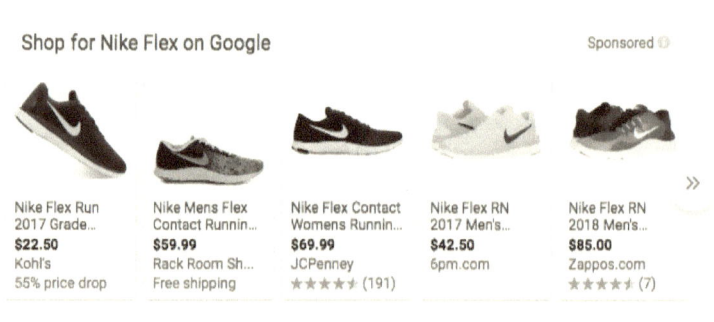

The Kohl's product ad in the example above, which is at an angle, would be more enticing and could generate more clicks.

Optimize the Google Merchant Center

Text ads typically allow you to determine how optimized your ads are by providing a quality score between one and ten. However, Google Shopping only provides the Merchant Center to help you determine if your ads are set up correctly. The Merchant Center is the ultimate resource to determine the accuracy and cleanliness of your data. Once you have uploaded your data into the feed, you should see all the disapprovals, warnings, and errors.

Issue	Country	Affected Items	% affected
Incorrect value [identifier exists]	United States	192 View samples	35.5%
Missing required attribute for apparel [size]	United States	26 View samples	4.8%
Missing required attribute for apparel [age group]	United States	25 View samples	4.6%
Missing required attribute for apparel [gender]	United States	25 View samples	4.6%
Automatic item updates active [price]	United States	6 View samples	1.1%
Missing required attribute for apparel [color]	United States	5 View samples	< 1%
Invalid value [color]	United States	1 View samples	< 1%

While your product ads can still show up in some searches if you do not optimize your Merchant Center, you will be at a disadvantage if your competitors have taken the time to optimize their Merchant Center accounts. Keep an eye out for the following warnings:

Account Level Warnings – This is the last thing that you want to see in your account and needs to be taken care of as soon as possible. Not doing so could result in your account getting shut down. This can include serious issues, such as verification that needs to be resolved immediately to keep your account active.

Feed Level Warnings – Google will verify your feed to ensure that all files are readable and have been set up correctly. You will receive warnings if there are any problems with your feed.

Item Level Warnings – Item level or SKU warnings tend to be at the specific product levels. The algorithm will scan your products and trigger a warning or recommendation if there are any missing attributes.

Regularly Update the Feed Data

To optimize your campaigns, you have to regularly update your shopping feed whenever your inventory levels, availability, or product prices change. For instance, if you had 600 items in stock last month and now have only 400, then you need to go into the data feed and update it. This ensures that you will not waste ad spending on products you no longer sell. This could result in 404 errors that may mess with the quality score of your feed. This can also cause your account to be suspended.

Analyze Ad Performance Data

Unlike traditional ads, you cannot bid on individual keywords in Google Shopping. Instead, Google will use product data from your ecommerce shop to determine which keywords and phrase your products show up for in searches. You do not have keywords to bid on in shopping only products.

HOW TO OPTIMIZE GOOGLE SHOPPING ADS

There are several strategies that you can apply to your shopping campaign. Below is a summary of each.

Automated Bidding for Google Shopping

Automated bidding is an effective strategy, particularly if you are running several campaigns at the same time. This allows Google's algorithms to learn and test your shopping ads and to discover the best bids for your products. The automated bidding system will use real-time trends and make changes to optimize your bids based on your chosen automated strategy.

When you set up Google Shopping ads, Google provides a range of automated bidding options that include maximizing clicks, enhanced PPC, Target ROAS, and rule-based bidding. Google has more detailed information about each strategy in their help guide.

Bidding and budget			
Bidding	Manual CPC		With "Manual CPC" bidding, you set your own maximum cost-per-click (CPC) for your ads.
	Change bid strategy ⓘ		
	Manual CPC ▼		Learn more
	☑ Help increase conversions with Enhanced CPC ⓘ		
			CANCEL SAVE

Maximize Clicks – The algorithm automatically sets bids so that your ads can receive as many clicks as they can within the target ad spend you set. This will make it possible to be within your target ad spend, even as you increase clicks to low-trafficked products. Be aware that that doesn't mean you will receive orders at a reasonable cost.

Enhanced CPC – The algorithm will adjust your manual bids to improve the probability of a click resulting in conversions. In doing so, it will enhance conversions while allowing you to control your bids.

Target ROAS – The algorithm will automatically set your bid to optimize conversion value while achieving a targeted return on ad spend (ROAS).

Rule-Based Bidding

It's important to understand that no matter how good automated strategies are, it is not necessary to automate *all* your ad strategies. A hybrid approach that includes human monitoring combined with automated strategies can be a very unimpactful strategy.

Some of the best rule-based strategies to adopt are:

- Bid increase rules
- Pull back on wasted ad spend
- Reduce bids on unprofitable terms
- Bump up products with zero impression

One of the biggest benefits in adopting rule-based bidding strategies is that it allows you to set thresholds. Through strategies such as threshold bidding, you can customize rules according to trends, ROI, impressions and conversions, which means you can make changes to your ads at scale. You can learn more about rule base bidding in Google's help section.

Optimize Product Images

Apart from the title, the image is one of the most important aspects in optimizing Google Shopping ads. For the person looking for a product on the search engine, it is just like window shopping at the mall, though the comparison and competition is on another level.

If you want to be successful with Google Shopping ads, you need to have high-quality images. You should also...

- Use white backgrounds.
- Try not use manufacturer/stock images.
- Use title and ALT tags in the image file.
- Use angles that bring out the product's best attributes.

Add Negative Keywords

Even though Google Shopping Ads do not depend on keywords as much as display or text ads do, you still need to optimize the account by removing negative keywords. Doing this will ensure that you do not appear for irrelevant keywords or keyword/phrases that convert at too high of a cost.

The "search terms" report should be your first stop when you are looking to optimize your ads. It gives you access to all of the search queries Google visitors were using before they were presented with ads.

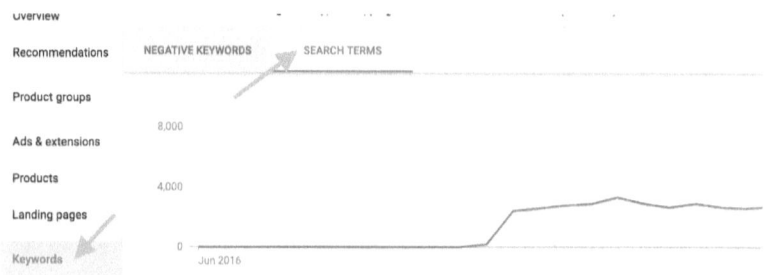

Once I enter the "search terms" section, I set a filter to ignore keywords that have converted. I then go through all the keywords and pause the irrelevant terms and any terms that have gone over my target cost per acquisition or average sales value. As an example; if the average order value for my products is $55 and I have key phrases in this "search term" report that have exceed $55, I would exclude them. You could keep them in and hope they will convert, but it most cases it will not.

You cannot view keywords for individual products, only all of the products collectively. Pay attention to the data, not your gut.

Even if a term is spot on to what you sell, if it is not converting, you will want to pause it.

Before pausing a highly relevant keyword or phrase, it's a good idea to Google that keyword or phrase and check to see which products of yours are showing up for that term. Is it the right product showing up for that term? If the answer is yes, then pause the keywords until you can determine why you are not converting. Is it due to a poor landing page design, slow load time, am item that is out of stock or another noticeable issue? If the answer is no, then you need to research and see why the wrong product is showing. Pause the incorrect ranking product and see if the correct one starts to show up.

Irrelevant Search Queries – Sort out your queries by impressions to get a list of all keywords you do not want your ads to be shown for. This may include color variations you do not sell, wrong size of clothes or any other irrelevant attribute.

Competitor Search Queries – These are product searches that involve competitor brand names combined with a product name. You may discover that your product is showing up when people search in Amazon, Target and other top brands. You will want to add those brands as negatives.

Use Promotion Codes

As I mentioned earlier in the shopping feed section, one of the most effective ways to stand out with shopping ads is by using promotions. If you have existing promotions, include them in your ads as they tend to trigger people's buying habits, resulting in higher click through rates at lower costs.

For instance, if you are running a promotion for your t-shirts at 30% off for a "spring sale", you can create a promotion code of SAVE30 on your website and include that in the shopping ad.

The first step is to create an attribute labeled "promotion ID," into which you can add the t-shirts that are on sale under the SAVE30 promotion code. Once you are done with that, go to your Merchant Center Account and navigate to "promotion" to create your ads.

Some promotions you can include in the product listing in Google Shopping include:

- Free shipping
- Brand specifies rebates
- Lowering the Free shipping threshold
- Buy One Get One or Buy One get the next at 70% off
- Tiered percentage discounts such as 10% off for orders greater than 50

In order to bid on individual products, you need to break out each product. If you keep the feed as it is, your bid will be the same for all products. You won't be able to bid on or pause individual products that perform poorly.

Breaking Out Products

Once you upload your feed into "Merchant Center," all of your products will be "lumped" together when you create and being to build out your shopping campaign within Google Ads. Remember, Google Merchant Center is where you upload your feed and Google Ads is where you go to set up your Google shopping campaigns. You can follow Google's instruction on how to do this or Google "Link Merchant Center To Google Ads."

Even if you have your products in categories, you won't be able to bid on each product individually right out of the gate. In order to see each product individually, you need to separate them from the main group. Click the pencil next to all products.

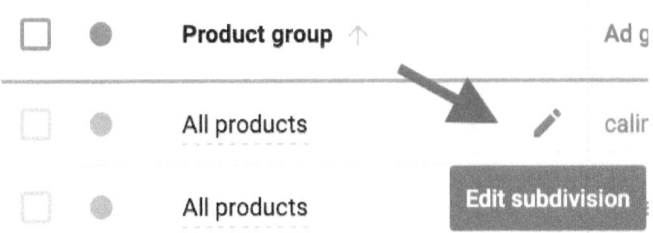

Select "Item ID," checkmark all the items and then click "add". Once you do that, you will be able to see each product in your ad group, making it much easier for you to pause and bid on individual products. If you don't break these products out, you'll have a much harder time trying to get a positive ROI in your account.

Select "all products" and click the pencil. You can then view a list of all your products. Click on "product ID," select them all and then click "save." You will now be able to bid and pause all the individual products with your feed.

In order to get the most out of your shopping campaigns, it is important that you maintain them on a regular basis.

Subdivide **All products** by: Item ID

Product group	Pro...	Clic...	Cos...
~~goods~~	1	0	$0.00
~~goods~~	1	0	$0.00
~~goods~~	1	0	$0.00
~~goods~~	1	0	$0.00
~~goods~~	1	0	$0.00
~~goods~~	1	0	$0.00

Bulk add values manually

In order to get the most out of your shopping campaigns, it is important that you maintain them on a regular basis. Increase bids when you need to, add negative keywords and pause products if they don't perform; not every product will be a successful product. Knowing when to pause a poor performing will save you money; you're not spending money on products that don't sell. This will allow you to spend more of your budget on products that actually perform.

A more advanced option is to group products by type. If you use a platform such as Shopify, your main category pages will also be categorized in your feed. It will look like this in Google Ads when you start creating your ad campaign.

What Are Google Smart Shopping Ads?

Google Shopping is a new type of Google Ads campaign that is intended to simplify advertising for ecommerce by making use of automated ad placement and bidding. This is beneficial for advertisers who find the process of setting up Google Shopping Ads too complex or those who do not have the time to set it up.

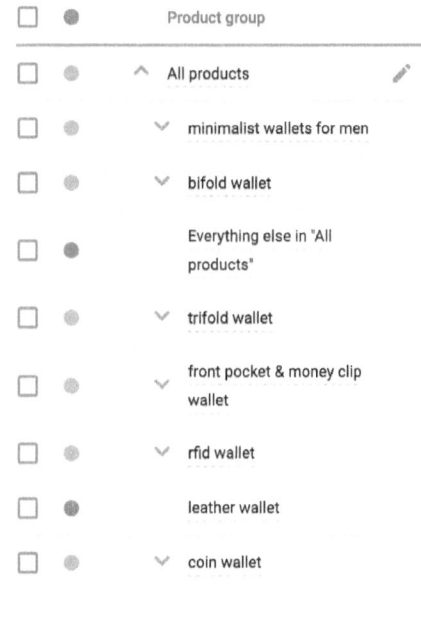

Smart Shopping Campaigns employ machine learning to make automated bids in certain circumstances when the searcher is likely to make a purchase. It then makes an approximate bid for the customer through unique contextual signals it applies for every auction. The algorithm typically uses a searchers historical browsing data and search queries to predict which products they are interested in.

On display networks, the system uses previous engagement data from similar websites or from your website to determine shoppers interests. With automated ad creation and placement, you receive more relevant clicks as ads are placed in ad spaces where they are likely to convert thus improving your conversions and ROI. The question you need to ask yourself is, "Should you use Google Smart Shopping?"

The Difference in Smart Shopping Campaigns

Smart Shopping Campaigns are similar to regular Google Shopping Campaigns except for simplification and automation. They maximize conversion value, simplify campaign management and expand the reach of your ads. The Smart Shopping campaigns also combine display remarketing with standard shopping in addition to automated ad placement and bidding.

Another new component introduced with Smart Shopping is the ability to serve both display ads and Product Shopping ads. You can also have your ads shown on display networks, search networks, Gmail and YouTube depending on how relevant they are to users. This may increase the ROI of your conversions.

How Does Google Smart Shopping Work?

Google will draw from the merchant-submitted product feed through the Google Merchant Center to create product ads. This is the same process that happens with conventional Google Shopping Ads and dynamic display ads.

The campaigns are set up from the Google Ads interface. Advertisers only need to supply creative for display ads, set budgets and optionally set a target ROAS goal to set up Smart Shopping. Google then uses automated bidding in addition to target ROAS goals to maximize conversion values for your campaigns.

What Is Smart Bidding?

Smart or automated bidding refers to how the Google algorithm uses machine learning and a variety of signals such as operating system, language, remarketing list, time of day, location, and device to determine the unique context of a user's search, ultimately setting a bid that is more likely to convert the client.

There are two types of automatic bidding:

Maximize Value – This makes it possible to generate as much revenue as possible from your budget. However, the setting means that you lose a lot of control over the ad spend.

Target Return On Ad Spend (ROAS) – The option focuses on maximizing conversion and revenue. However, it does provide greater control over the ad spend. This is better for campaigns with strict ROIs, as it will provide better value.

Who Can Use Smart Shopping Campaigns?

Before you can use Google Smart Shopping there are several requirements you have to meet. You need to have:

- A Google Ads account

- An audience of at least 100 users or more

- A Google Merchant Center Account

- Shopping Campaigns that had over 20 conversions in the past 45 days

- A product data feed that you have uploaded and gotten approved in your account

- Tagged the site for dynamic remarketing
- A conversion tracking tag installed on the website
- A remarketing global site tag on the website
- Tracking for transaction-specific conversion values

Many advertisers set up smart campaigns as soon as they set up their account. However, without any data, your campaigns will likely fail.

How to Set Up Smart Shopping Campaigns

Smart Shopping combines display marketing and conventional Google Shopping. As such, if you are running any of these you need to pause them before you target the same products using Smart Shopping.

The procedure to set up Smart Shopping Campaigns is as follows:

- Log into Google Ads and create a new campaign.
- Click on "shopping" in the dashboard to select it, then click on "sales" as the campaign goal.
- Click on the Merchant Center account you intend to use and then select the target country for the campaign.
- Lastly, check the box beside "Smart Shopping Campaign."
- Name your campaign and assign a budget.

- Set a Target ROAS (this is optional.. However, note that if you do not set the ROAS, the algorithm will default to maximize conversion bidding, which you do not want to implement as you will not have any conversion data in the account.

- Add the business logo for use in display networks. Finally, add the completed URL, description as well as a long and short headline.

Note that the algorithm will include all the products that you included in the product feed unless you specify that you do not want them included. The system works best when the algorithm has access to all of your products.

Best Practice for Smart Shopping Ads

There are several tips and tricks that will help to improve the performance of Smart Shopping Ads:

- Keep in mind that the default setting for campaigns is to maximize conversion value and conversions according to the budget. The goal is to provide the highest ROAS and highest conversion values.

- It is best to use conventional shopping campaigns with a maximization bidding setting to fulfill remarketing and conversion requirements.

- Allow some time for the Google algorithms to collect data on your customers. 15-20 days is sufficient, meaning that you should start seeing good results in two to three weeks. Depending on conversion volume, the period could be longer or shorter.

- Once you implement Smart Shopping campaigns, track your performance and measure how each campaign performs once and compare them to the traditional Google Shopping campaigns you were running before.

- Update your feeds regularly! Optimize images, descriptions, and titles across all the campaigns.

- Target a few specific product groups when you are starting and continue to run the rest on the traditional Google Shopping campaign. This will ensure you do not experience a sudden interruption ion performance on your eCommerce store.

Pros of Google Smart Shopping

Shopping campaigns used to be complex and tedious, even for the experts. Smart Shopping campaigns provide a range of features to revolutionize how consumers shop and ecommerce businesses advertise on Google.

Smart Shopping Allows You to Set "Acquire New Customers" As A Smart Goal

Rather than just tracking conversions and clicks, Smart Shopping makes it possible to track new customers while providing insights that can help you make decisions to drive more sales. For instance, with the data you get, you can refine your targeting to improve your ROI.

Ecommerce Businesses Can Automate Advertising Campaigns

Setting up advertising on Google Shopping may take too much time or cost a lot of money. With Smart Shopping, the process is less complex and less time-consuming. Most aspects of a campaign, from targeting, creatives and bidding, can be automated. This makes advertising more efficient for businesses to run advertising campaigns.

Cons of Smart Shopping Campaigns

While Smart Shopping campaigns can be very effective, they also have some limitations. Some of these limitations include:

Ad Scheduling – You do not have the option of scheduling when your ads will run, as the algorithm makes all the decisions. Until the algorithm learns which are the best hours, you will lose money to bad scheduling decisions.

Audience Targeting – Google will select the customers that it thinks are best for you.

Bid Adjustments – Adjusting and optimizing can significantly improve the performance of a campaign and improve the ROI on budget spend. With Smart Shopping, there is no option to adjust your bids.

- **Device Targeting** – Some businesses do better on mobile while others do better on desktop, but Smart Shopping does not allow you to decide what devices to run your ads on, thus possibly wasting money.

- **Granular Reporting** – It is impossible to determine where your sales are coming from, as Smart Shopping combines all of Gmail, YouTube, Shopping and Display data.

- **Lack of Negative Keywords** – It is not possible to set negative keywords in Smart Shopping. They can be very important in enhancing the efficiency of a campaign, but by not having this feature there are some inherent inefficiencies in Smart Shopping as there would inevitably be for irrelevant search traffic.

- **Location Targeting** – While you can target a country, you cannot exclude or target specific regions, causing you to pay for irrelevant traffic.

- **Network Placements** – Businesses are not allowed to decide where their ads will appear, making performance measuring difficult. For instance, Search and Gmail will overall be better when you optimize for conversions, while you will typically get lower conversions and CTRs on Display Networks. Since you cannot opt-out of networks that do not work for you, you are likely to pay for unqualified or poorly converting traffic.

Should You Use Smart Shopping Campaigns?

In my experience, using an automated strategy (Smart Shopping) tends to perform worse as time goes by. You're giving up control to a system that will try to drive more sales by allowing your products to show for broader–and in many cases, irrelevant– terms. In the end, it's your decision. If you are short on time and want to test using Smart Shopping on a few products, go for it.

Minimum Amount for Google Ads Campaign?

While setting your own budgets in Google Ads is great, you still need to have a reasonable size budget. Many small businesses will throw a tiny amount of money at advertising, hoping to magically get all the data they need to determine the future success of their account.

If your average CPC (cost per click) is $3 and you have a $300 per month budget, that comes out to be roughly $10, or 3 clicks, a day. Your campaign could run out of funds within an hour or two. How can you expect to generate sales when only a few of your products are being shown?

As I mentioned earlier, your products will show up for irrelevant terms, it's just part of collecting data and managing your account. If you combine irrelevant keywords and the amount of time your products are showing, how long do you think it will take for you to collect the data you need? Days, weeks or months?

You also need to take into account that your ads will start at the same time and run at roughly the same time every day. What if you convert more in the evenings then you do in the mornings? You'll never find out; your budget will never get you that far in a day.

Be realistic with your budget. If you want to test a small number of products you can, but just be sure you have enough budget to run the campaign 24 hours a day for at least 30 days. Otherwise, you're wasting your money and time. If your budget is small, you have a few options:

- Run only a few select products at a time.
- Trying running shopping campaigns on Bing.
- Save your money until you have enough to run a campaign for a full month.

In the many years of managing shopping campaigns, small budgets are almost always guaranteed to fail since you won't be able to collect enough data. Especially if the campaign is being managed poorly. Also, if your CPC is close to your daily budget, Google may not run your ads at all.

Bing ads mimic a lot of the same features and functions as Google Ads. You can easily use this book to manage your shopping ads in Bing as well, and if your budget is small, you might want to start there first.

ECOMMERCE BLOGGING

What will you learn from this section?

This section will be your guide with actionable items to help you increase the organic traffic you receive from search engines. Some of what I will cover includes:

- How to conduct keyword research without any paid tools.
- Why traditional link building isn't necessary to rank content.
- How to connect Google analytics to search console.
- How to set up ecommerce tracking in Google analytics.
- How to create Google analytics reports instantly.
- The one important item that can cripple a websites ability to drive traffic, even with tons of great content.
- A guide to creating, optimizing and tracking your content creation and growth.

- How to get more content out of the content you create.

...and much more.

Essentially, the above is everything you need to start planning and creating your content. While most businesses understand that content is important, they fall short in understanding what type of content they should be creating that will turn visitors into buyers.

What Should You Write About?

As a shopping business, your blog posts should cover questions that people have about your products, such as comparisons of similar products on your site (or your competitor's) and possibly review type queries. These topics could be directly about your products or the problems your product solves. When it comes to buying products, people who know which product they want to buy will use different keywords then those searching for a solution or conducting research. Some searchers may be conducting research on a particular product to learn more about it and its features, comparison shopping or just to research more about a product they are thinking about buying.

This could also be a free solution to a problem they currently have before they resort to paying for one. The ideal strategy is to show up for all of these types of searches. This guide will help you easily identify which phrases to target, how to track the content you create and when to make changes to this content.

For example, let's say you sell a product that eliminates pet odors. You may decide to write a blog post about the "Five Ways to Eliminate Dog Odors at Home." You could go into detail on the different ways people can eliminate these types of odors from their homes. Why would you want someone to make something at home instead of buying your product? The answer is simple; the searcher is looking for an easy and quick way to solve their problem. Your goal is to serve that need.

The article can contain your product as one of the solutions in the article. The reader may try other remedies first, but if they fail or if they find it to be too troublesome to create these concoctions, they may be more likely to use your product, especially once you go into how much research and testing went into your product.

Additionally, if you sell sports equipment, there is virtually an unlimited amount of content you could write about. "Choosing the Right Baseball Helmet," or "Which is Better, a Wooden or an Aluminum Bat?" Your article will help the searcher decide which is better. Hopefully, you've included links to your wooden and aluminum bats within the article so that if the reader is ready to purchase, they can easily click over to your product page and buy. This is also content that bloggers tend to link to. I'll explain more about links later.

How to Conduct Keyword Research?

You're probably thinking you need to use a paid tool to do this research, but you don't. At best, most tools are estimates of what people are searching for. Plus, we aren't looking to rank for keywords, but key phrases and questions.

The best place for that is Google search. As you type inside Google's search bar, you'll notice Google will try and guess what you're looking, for based on data they've collected. Let's take motorcycle buying, for example. Here are some of the search suggestions Google shows me:

how to buy a moto

how to buy a **motorcycle**
how to buy a **motorcycle helmet**
how to buy a **motorhome**
how to buy a **motorcycle on craigslist**
how to buy a **motorcycle online**
how to buy a **motorcycle without a title**
how to buy a **motorcycle with a lien**
how to buy a **motorcycle out of state**
how to buy a **motorcycle with bad credit**
how to buy a **motorcycle from a dealer**

Report inappropriate predictions

Not a bad start. I see a few good topics. What if I perform my search using "buy a motorcycle" and place my cursor before the word "buy" and hit the space bar?

buy a motorcycle

buy a motorcycle
should i buy a motorcycle
best time to buy a motorcycle
can i buy a motorcycle **without a license**
how to buy a motorcycle **from a private seller**
best time of year to buy a motorcycle
where to buy a motorcycle **helmet**
can you buy a motorcycle **with a permit**
buy a motorcycle **online**
best time to buy a motorcycle **from a dealer**

You now have additional ideas for creating content. You can mix and match different terms and words to come up with an almost endless list of topics to write about. Some of these questions could be answered in one blog post, while others could be standalone "pillar" posts. "How to Buy a Motorcycle

Online" And "How to Buy a Motorcycle From Craigslist" could be addressed in one article. The same could be said for "Where to Buy a Motorcycle Helmet" and "How to Buy a Motorcycle Helmet." While "How to Buy A Motorcycle Online" could be a standalone post. This would most likely be a pillar post, possibly 3,000 words or more. There is so much information and research that would go into this topic that you could probably write an eBook on it.

What if you sold leather wallets? How hard is it to come up with content ideas? I went to Google and typed "how to" with a space in between each phrase, and then typed "leather wallet." Here are my results:

how to leather wallet

how to **clean** leather wallet
how to **make a** leather wallet
how to **shrink** leather wallet
how to **dry** leather wallet
how to **restore** leather wallet
how to **soften** leather wallet
how to **clean** leather wallet **at home**
how to **wash** leather wallet
how to **clean** leather wallet **fossil**
how to **take care of** leather wallet

Many of these suggestions are good blog topics. "How to Clean a Leather Wallet" is a great idea, especially if you sell cleaning products for leather. Even if you don't sell cleaning supplies, this is still a good blog post to write. A reader may decide cleaning their old wallet isn't worth the hassle and buying a new one is better–maybe because you suggest it in your article. When it comes to how you search for writable topics, you are only limited by your creativity.

This strategy is one of the best ways to discover content ideas. I use this tactic when creating content for myself or for my clients. It's easy, simple and effective. I would also recommend researching to see which sites rank for these phrases and questions. If you see forums as search results, there is a good chance you could easily outrank them with long and informative content.

Another tool you can use is Answer the Public, which allows you to enter search terms or questions into its search engine. The results are questions similar to or related to the keywords you entered. In this example, I entered the question "How to buy a motorcycle?" You can see that the questions are grouped by "why," "when," "are," "will," "which" and "can" related inquiries.

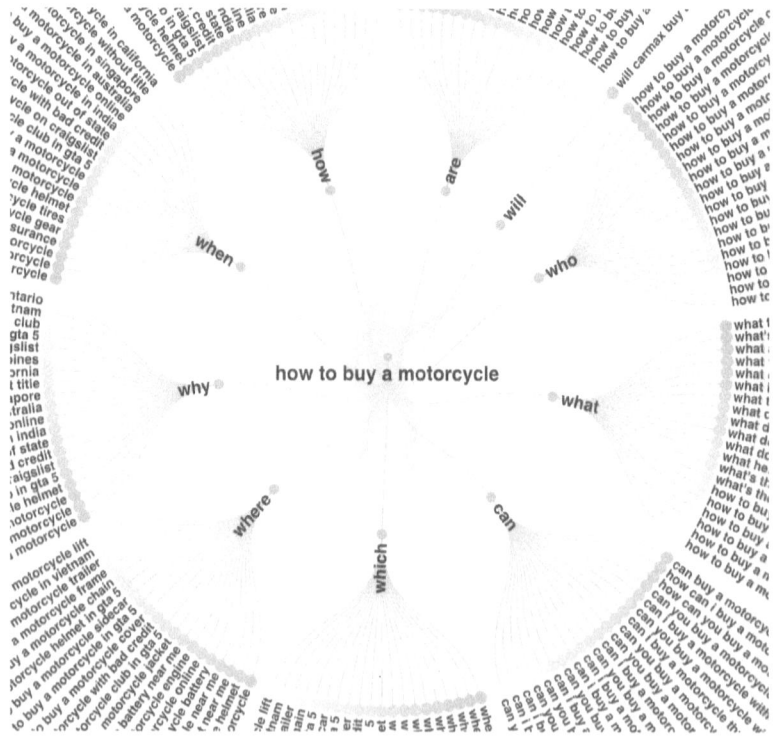

You can use these questions as part of the content you create, or it may foster ideas for future content. You don't always need to word your content in the form of a question. You could take this example "how to buy a motorcycle helmet" and change it to "choosing the right motorcycle helmet," which also ranks on the first page of Google when you search using the word "buy."

You can perform different searches to uncover additional ways to word content, to rank it for a similar term or phrase. Be sure, to review the websites that already rank in Google for those terms to get a sense of how the content is written. If the question you're answering appears on the webpage, you may want to include it in your content. You probably should if it's not in the title of your page.

PRO TIP: Another way to find good topics to write about is to monitor the blogs of your competitor's for ideas or use a service like Buzzsumo to help you identify popular articles and topics.

How Much Content Should You Write?

In my experience, if you want to rank well, your content should be at least 1,000-3,000 words. However, the content shouldn't be boring, repetitive or copied content from other sites. It's important that your content not be written attempting to "optimize" for any particular key phrases. Your writing has a purpose and your content is going to be filled with as much useful information as possible, including photos, videos and links to other resources.

In order for this method to work, especially on a new website, you have to be able to create 4-8 pieces of unique content a month for at least 6-10 months; even more content is better. You won't need to create as much content after the first 8 months or so, but you should continue to have a steady schedule of content.

Why Is This So Important?

Google will be looking at not only the length of the content you write but how much of it you write and its overall usefulness. Google isn't going to rank a site with just one blog post on it. You need to show Google that you are an expert, authoritative and trustworthy (EAT.) Creating regular content that answers questions and helps solve problems is a good way to do that. This also works if your site is focused on selling a particular product or products in a specific category. In other words, if you sold only sports equipment, then you can build up your reputation as an expert in that field. If your site sells home goods, electronics and furniture, it will be hard to be an expert on many different departments on one site.

What Type of Information Should Be Included in Your Content?

The purpose of your content is to educate the readers. You can do so by adding:

- Important statistics
- Supporting images
- Adding video, audio or presentations
- Links in content to relevant products

- Quotes from experts or famous people
- Links to tools and other valuable resources

How to Structure Your Content

- Start with your lead paragraph. This paragraph can reaffirm what the title of the. article suggests, what the rest of the article will entail or what readers will learn.

- Know your audience and why they are seeking out the content you wrote.

- Keep paragraphs short and use images, as long stretches of content can appear. boring to a reader, especially on long blog posts.

- Keep from using too much industry jargon. The tone should be light and come from a place of experience.

- Use real examples and follow a clear logical progression.

- Have someone proofread your content to ensure it makes sense and has a natural flow to it. You can even use a free writing tool such as Grammarly. There is also a free browser plugin that integrates with Google Docs.

- The closing should be a summary of what was in the article. If you're selling a product or service that relates to the article, you can add a call to action.

Incoming links to ecommerce sites can be difficult to achieve, especially for sites that don't sell a unique product. However, creating content that answers questions and provides useful information can acquire links and social shares, if crafted well.

Experiment with the types of articles you write (tips, how-to, comparisons, etc.)

Use analytics to monitor blog post traffic over time to see which drives the most organic traffic. Content that drives a lot of organic traffic and sales could be a candidate for a follow-up post, piggybacking off of the feedback on the original posts that answer questions or solves problems.

> **PRO TIP:** Allow comments on your blog posts to add engagement. Posts that have engagement tend to be shared more. Plus, the comments may provide you with content for a future piece of content. Give it a try!

A Working Example

I realize that without visual examples, it's hard to see what the possible results are for all of the content you will be creating. While planning out this book, I decided to build a complete B2B website in a very competitive space–web hosting. While this is more of a service-type business, it does require research on the user's end and the site offers service products and services.

In June, I began writing content and I would create a few pieces a week over the next few months. I did not tweak any copy or do any link building.

The below graph shows the average position of my content. As you can see, over time the average position in Google improved.

Even though I'm collectively averaging a position of 80, I do have some phrases on the first page of Google. I also have phrases and terms that don't rank at all on Google.

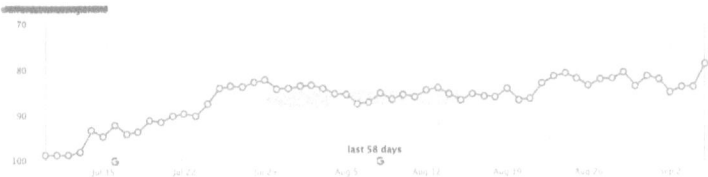

It's important to note that without making any on-page changes or updates from when I first uploaded my content rankings improved. Are these numbers groundbreaking? No, but what they show is proof of concept. A brand-new site with no backlinks and well-written content can produce decent results. There is more work to do here and this is only just a few months into creating content. The results for you may vary. As I stated earlier, don't expect any movement for 5 months or more.

> **PRO TIP:** Don't be afraid to link to sites that you reference as sources within your content. This helps add credibility to your content and shows that time and research has gone into creating the content. Just be sure to not link too often within one piece of content and to always have links that leave your site open in a new window.

HOW TO TURN YOUR CONTENT INTO A SALES TOOL

Let's take a look at types of baseball bats.

types of baseball bats	🔍

People also ask

What type of baseball bat hits the farthest?	⌄
Which baseball bat is the best?	⌄
What kind of bats are used in Little League?	⌄
What bat material is the best?	⌄

Feedback

If you're comparing baseball bats, you can list on the page all the different types of bats with photos that then link to the co-ordinating product page. Or, if you are comparing the different types of bat materials, you can link each material to the section of your site that sells bats in that category.

If your post answers several questions, place those as headers inside your piece and answer them in the corresponding content.

For example, if you're writing content that's more of a "how-to," you may be able to answer several questions within one post. However, I would avoid going after "review" articles unless there aren't many sites that rank for that particular phrase.

Images help break up blocks of content. Videos can help extend the "time on page," a ranking signal to Google. Google looks at how long a visitor spends on your page. The longer someone spends on your site, the stronger the signal is to Google that your content is resonating with searchers.

The opposite can be said as well. If a user leaves your page and goes to another page, they spend more time on that site. The video within your content doesn't need to be yours, it just has to support your content. Don't feel the need to create your own video for the sake of placing it in your post. You could also embed an infographic or audio from a podcast or presentation.

Once you've compiled a list of all the possible questions and phrases you want to try and rank for, you will need to work on an editorial calendar. It will help you plan and stay focused on the goal of creating content for the purpose of driving traffic.

PRO TIP: While gaining followers on social media is a good metric to use, I recommend placing social profile links in the footer of the site and not the header. If you give users too many calls to action, they tend to either choose the least important one or none at all.

HOW TO OPTIMIZE FOR FEATURED SNIPPETS

What Are Featured Snippets?

Featured snippets are search results that are shown on the top of or in between Google's organic search results, right below the paid ads box. Featured snippets attempt to answer a user's question right away (also known as "answer boxes.")

Being featured in snippets increases the click-through to your site, your brand recognition and exposure. Large snippets are pulled from paragraphs. When you are researching which phrases and questions you want to write about, take a look at which sites rank for those question related snippets.

Google	adwords account suspended	

Has Your **Adwords Account** Been **Suspended**? If you violate any Google's terms of service, advertising policies, or engage in suspicious activity with payment or billing issues, your **Adwords account** gets **suspended**. A **suspended** or banned **account** cannot be allowed to run any kind of campaigns. Sep 11, 2016

Reasons Your Adwords Account Can Be Suspended And How To ...
https://4pointdigital.com › 2016/09/11 › reasons-your-adwords-account-can-...

About Featured Snippets   Feedback

You can also see what other related questions were asked, including some of those questions within your own content. Take note of how long the answers are and if they are in the form of a paragraph, bullets or a table.

According to SEMrush, the average length of a featured snippet is between 40-50 words. Use this range when writing answers to the questions you are answering within your blog post. Bullets points also get picked up quite a bit and should be used as well.

People also ask

Why is my Google AdWords account suspended?

How do I reactivate my AdWords account?

How to reactivate your account

1. Sign in to your Google Ads account.
2. Click the tools icon in the upper right-hand corner.
3. Under 'Set-up', click Preferences.
4. Click the Account Status section to expand it.
5. Click Reactivate my account.

Reactivate a cancelled Google Ads account - New - Google Ads Help
https://support.google.com › google-ads › answer › co=ADWORDS.IsAWN...

Search for: How do I reactivate my AdWords account?

What does account suspended mean?

How do I Unsuspend my Google account?

How do I contact Google AdWords?

PRO TIP: You don't need to rank number one in Google to have your content featured in a snippet, you just have to be in the top ten. You also want to have the answer to questions placed inside of tables. Placing content in tables will make it easier for Google to pull your content into search results.

SHOULD YOU WRITE ALL THE CONTENT YOURSELF?

In my opinion, no one is going to take the time to write content with as much passion or research as you will. However, writing a lot of content takes time and effort. If you can find a decent writer for a good portion of the work, it will make your life easier. In most cases, a 1,000-word article will cost around $35.

It's important to find writers who have similar writing styles as you do. Create a few articles yourself and send them to the writers you are looking to try out. Give them a sense of how you write and what you need. You may need to tweak some of the content that they write for you, but overall the content will be written the way you want it to be. There are several places you can have content written for you at a fair price. The two I use most are iWriter and Upwork.

iWriter will allow you to create a project at the level of quality you want the content to be written. If you don't like the article, you can reject it. You can even choose to reject the writer and prevent them from bidding on your jobs. Once you find a writer or two that you like, you can then "favorite" them and assign articles to them.

Upwork allows you to place a listing that writers can bid on. You can review a person's past work. However, once you go with them, you cannot reject the content. You can, of course, ask for changes to be made. In my experience, iWriter works better for me and the content I want to create. I suggest you try both and see which works best for you.

On-Page Blog Optimization

What Is A Title Tag?

A title tag is the text that shows up in the tab of your browser at the top line of a search result (see the red box below.)

> Trump accuses Google of 'rigged' search results for news - NBC N...
> https://www.nbcnews.com › tech › trump-accuses-google-rigged-search-re... ▼
> Aug 28, 2018 · **Trump** attacked Google, alleging that its news results show too few ... Joe Balestrino, an independent search-engine-optimization expert, told ...

What Title Tags Are Not

Title tags are not a place where you want to spam keywords, repeat terms too many times or try to target several different keywords/phrases in. The title tells Google and readers what the page is about. The title tag should summarize what the page entails while also using your targeted phrases.

What Is a Meta Description?

A meta description is what shows up under the title of the results in search engines. The goal of this is to provide the "right" information to get searchers to click on your listing. This is your opportunity to craft a message that will support the title of the page with a call to action. If you use your targeted keywords for the page in question in the meta description, Google will bold them to show the searcher that the content contains words that they just used to perform their search.

Depending on the search term your post shows, Google may pull a snippet from your post in an attempt to show the searcher some relative content. In those cases, there isn't much you can do. Below is a sample of a good meta description that includes a call to action (red box.) The searched keywords are bolded (red arrows) within the meta description.

Reasons Why Your Site Is Indexed But Not Ranking & How To Fix It
https://joebalestrino.com › why-your-site-is-indexed-but-not-ranking ▾
Aug 7, 2019 - Don't know why your site is indexed but not ranking? It could be one of many reasons. Read this article and find out those reasons and how to ...

What Are H1 Tags and How to Leverage Them?

An H1 tag is the first header on a page. In many cases, this is an exact copy of what's in the title tag. However, seasoned SEO's don't like to use the same wording in the title tag as they use for the H1 tag.

We want to be sure searches see their question when they Google it. However, on the page, I may want to use my target keyword in another way. Let's say my long-term goal is to rank for "fixing a flat tire on a motorcycle." My title tag may read "How to Easily Fix a Flat On a Motorcycle," which includes my long-term key phrase and encompasses a long-tailed similar and relevant search.

My H1 tag might read, "How to Repair a Flat Tire on a Motorcycle." Why the switch? The title tag confirms the questions and the H1 tag confirms the answer. Plus, I want to try and rank for "How to Repair a Flat Tire on a Motorcycle" as well. Google knows that repair and fix are the same. However, I noticed that if I use each term once in the title and once in the page header, I have a better chance of ranking for both.

You could also have an article titled (title tag) "How to Repair a Motorcycle Tire in 5 Easy Steps" and the H1 title could read "How to Change a Motorcycle Tire Easily." You can test and play with the two. Optimizing doesn't stop after you write the article; you may need to go back and make tweaks over time. This is why keeping notes and using tracking tools are important.

Do you need to change the title tag and headers to be successful? No, you do not. This is more of an advanced method, as it is not required to achieve good results.

PRO TIP: If possible, do *not* include the date of the article in the URL string. Example; abc.com/08/12/201/article-title. We want this content we're writing to be "evergreen" and not have an expiration date. Google can use the date in the URL to gauge its freshness.

HOW TO SET UP SEARCH CONSOLE & GOOGLE ANALYTICS

If you're not tracking and measuring your traffic, you will have no idea how much traffic you're receiving, or which pieces of content are doing better than others. These are free tools that you can set up easily using a WordPress plugin or by adding some code to all of your website's pages.

Analytics is a vital tool for every website owner. While many site owners add analytics tracking to their site, very few set up their account well enough to measure vital data.

In order to know how to grow your business, you need to first understand where the traffic is coming from, which sources drive the most revenue/traffic and which pieces of content perform the best. While Google stopped sharing keyword data within Google analytics years ago, if you set up search console you can link the two and pull some of that keyword data into analytics.

Search console is a very useful tool as Google provides website owners with important information about how Google views the site. This could be in the form of reports, errors, penalties, and sitemap issues. However, for our purpose, we want to be able to see keywords and the pages that drive organic traffic from Google. We will then import that data into analytics for easy reporting.

There are other important metrics you should be reviewing in analytics and I've included them within this guide. I've also included some easy to implement reporting dashboards to help you find that important data easily. By simply placing a small snippet of JavaScript code on your site, you will be able to collect and track user behavior, providing details such as:

- Bounce rates
- Session duration
- Pages they visited
- New and repeat visitors
- User affinity/interests' categories
- Traffic sources (social media, search)
- Demographics such as gender and age
- The location of the user including country and city
- Devices they are using including browser/operating system

With custom configuration, you can collect other information such as plays, clicks on content, the path to purchase funnels, contact form and goals, amongst others.

HOW TO SETUP GOOGLE ANALYTICS AND GOOGLE SEARCH CONSOLE

Google Analytics and Google Search Console both provide tons of data on the visitors to your site, as well as how they got there. One of the setbacks to using these two platforms was that you had to log into each account separately to get the information. However, in 2016 Google made it possible to connect Search Console to Google Analytics and analyze consolidated data without having to log into separate accounts. Here is how it is done:

Submit Your Site to Google Search Console

You need to submit and verify your website in Google Search Console. If you have already done that, you can move to the next step. If not, check out this link on how to submit your website to Google Search Console.

Google Analytics

If you have already set up Google Analytics, you can go on to verify ownership of the website using Google Analytics as long as:

1. You are using the asynchronous version of the tracking code.

2. The tracking code is placed in the <head> section of the page.

3. You have edit permissions for the Google Analytics property.

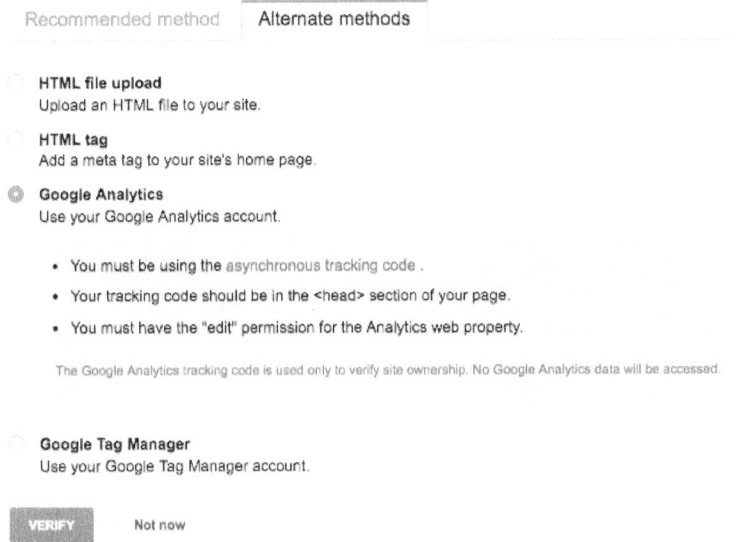

If you are using this method, you will have to install Google Analytics directly and not use the tag manager. If you will be using tag manager follow the instructions below.

Google Tag Manager

If you will be using Tag Manager, all you need to do is install the container snippet on your page. Note that you will need to have the "manage" permissions for the website's Tag Manager container.

> **Google Tag Manager**
> Use your Google Tag Manager account.
> - You must be using the container snippet.
> - You must have the "manage" permission for the Tag Manager container.
>
> The Google Tag Manager container ID is used only to verify site ownership. No Google Tag Manager data will be accessed.

HTML File Upload

You could also prove ownership of the site by uploading a verification code inside an HTML file.

> **HTML file upload**
> Upload an HTML file to your site.
> 1. **Download** this HTML verification file. [google53b458b8e8839518.html]
> 2. **Upload** the file to http://www.chrisgoddard.me/
> 3. **Confirm** successful upload by visiting http://www.chrisgoddard.me/google53b458b8e8839518.html in your browser.
> 4. **Click** Verify below.
>
> To stay verified, don't remove the HTML file, even after verification succeeds.

Once you have downloaded the file, you can upload it to the website where it will be accessible from the root. Note that the file should not be removed as Google will be periodically checking for verification.

HTML Tag

- **HTML tag**
  Add a meta tag to your site's home page.

  1. Copy the meta tag below, and paste it into your site's home page. It should go in the <head> section, before the first <body> section.

  ```
  <meta name="google-site-verification" content="RmLiO211RTKluwbolpfSXO_WjqWLKpj-S4vHikPAyCE" />
  ```

  ▶ Show me an example
  2. Click **Verify** below.

  To stay verified, don't remove the meta tag, even after verification succeeds.

You can also use the HTML tag to verify your website if your CMS allows you to add custom meta tags. This may be very convenient if you are using CMSs such as WordPress, as there are many plugins you can use to add the verification tag.

DNS

This is the recommended way of verifying your site since it does not need hosting, your website or another dependency to become verified. Using DNS and Search console, you will add a TXT record to the DNS records to verify the site.

```
google-site-verification=RmLiO211RTKluwbolpfSXO_WjqWLKpj-S4vHikPAyCE
```

This is the best way of verifying, as it means you cannot lose verification when the site is down, or the snippet is accidentally deleted. If you have access to DNS records, you should definitely verify using this method.

LINKING GOOGLE ANALYTICS WITH GOOGLE SEARCH CONSOLE

Choosing Analytics Property

Log in to the Google Analytics property and then click on the "Admin" tab. Click on the "cog" and the Property Settings to select the property you want to integrate.

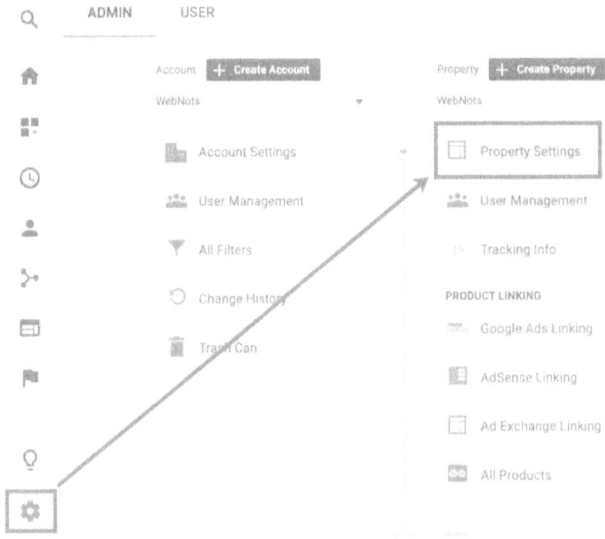

Choosing Search Console Property

A new screen will pop up on the right with details of the selected website. Scroll down to the Search Console tab and click on "Adjust Search Console."

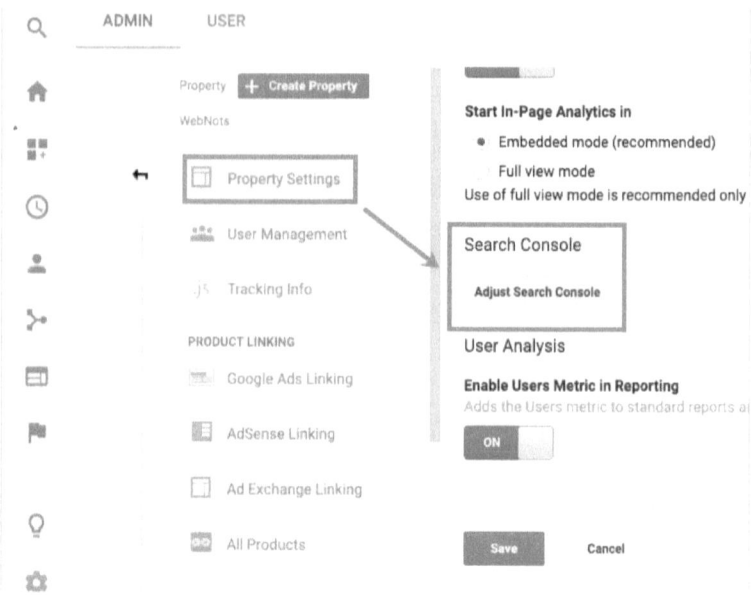

The Search Console settings will look as they do below. Click the button "add" link.

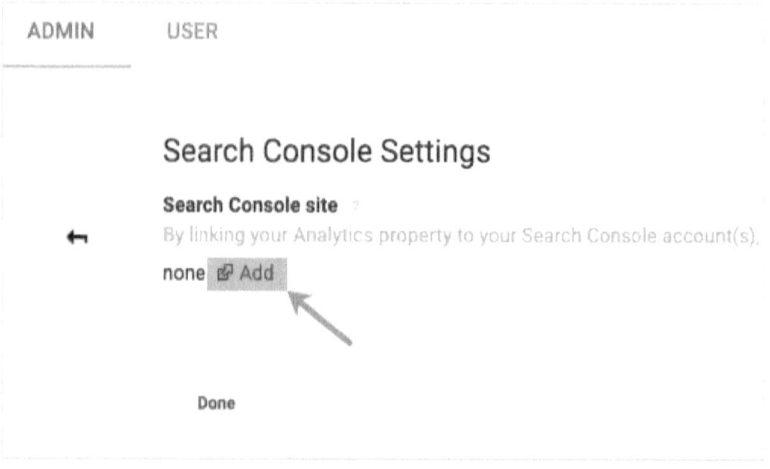

Linking Properties

You should see all the websites in the Search Console Account in your Google Analytics. Find the website not already linked to another Analytics Account. Mistakenly linking an already linked account will mean that the integration with the other Analytics property will be automatically removed.

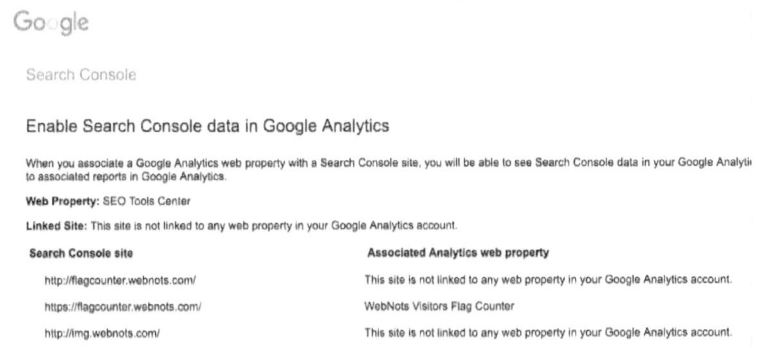

Click on the property you intend to integrate and then click "Save." Click on the "OK" prompt to confirm.

Head to the analytics homepage and refresh it. You should see whether the Search Console property has been integrated into the Google analytics account.

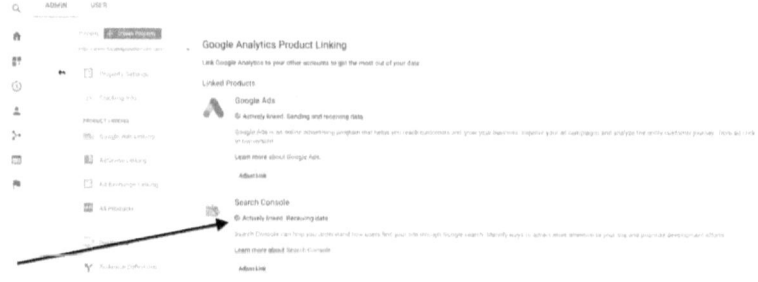

HOW TO FIND GOOGLE SEARCH CONSOLE DATA IN GOOGLE ANALYTICS

Once you have integrated Search Console with Google Analytics, you can have all your Search Console data right in Google Analytics. To find this data click on the scroll down and click "Acquisition." On the following menu, click "Search Console."

You can now access information on Landing Pages. You can get information on what pages people from different traffic are going to when visiting your website. Simply click the page URL and you should see what search queries are bringing in traffic to a given page.

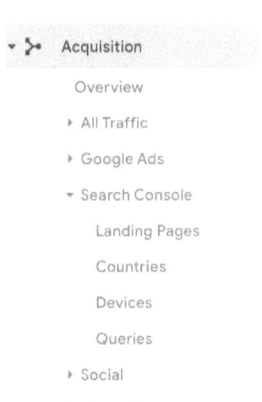

Countries

You get the information on which countries are bringing in traffic to your website. Simply click on the country to see the queries bringing in traffic to a given page.

Devices Report

This report will tell you what devices visitors use to access your website, whether it be desktop, tablet or mobile. All you need to do is click on a "Device" category and you will have sorted device-based information on the most visited pages.

Queries

The queries report gives information on the search terms that are bringing in traffic on the website. You can also get the average ranking positions on Google search for the given terms.

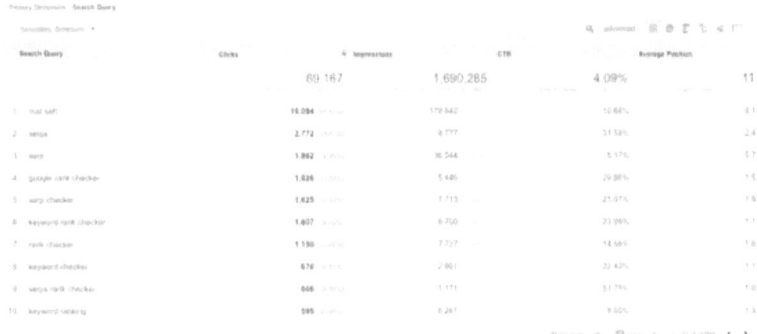

HOW TO TRACK REVENUE AND LEADS IN GOOGLE ANALYTICS

The most important metric for a business is revenue, which comes from the traffic the site receives. To track leads and revenue, you need to set up goals in Google Analytics.

Identifying Goals

Goals are the activities that have an impact on the revenue of the website which makes them very critical to track. Goals typically depend on what you are trying to accomplish. For instance, some common goals that you could track for your business include:

- Phone calls
- Session duration
- eBook downloads

- Newsletter sign-ups
- Leads (contact forms)

Every goal that you set needs to have some monetary value to the business, such as a newsletter subscriber being worth $1, a $40 phone call or a new lead worth $30. By assigning a value, it is possible to understand the value of different channels and marketing efforts.

How to Set Up Goals in Google Analytics

Create a New Goal

Click on the Admin tab which will open the page with the three columns: View, Property, and Account.

Look for the heading "Goals" in the "View" column and click on it.

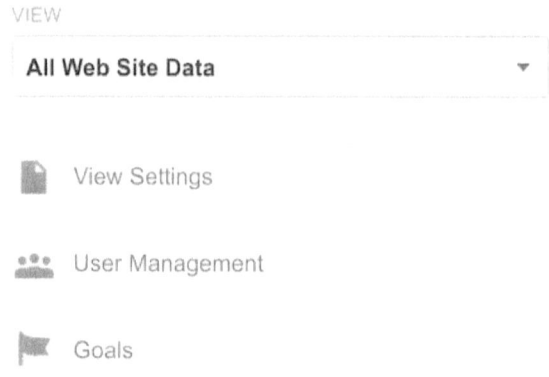

On the goals page, scroll down to the bottom of the page and click on the "New Goal" button.

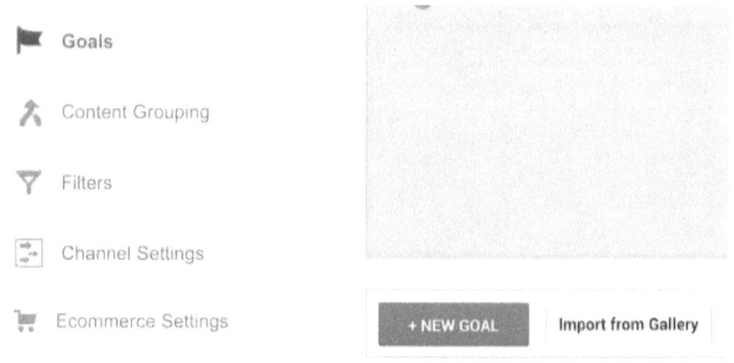

Choose Goal Setup

Google Analytics comes with three pre-configured templates; Inquiry, Acquisition, and Revenue.

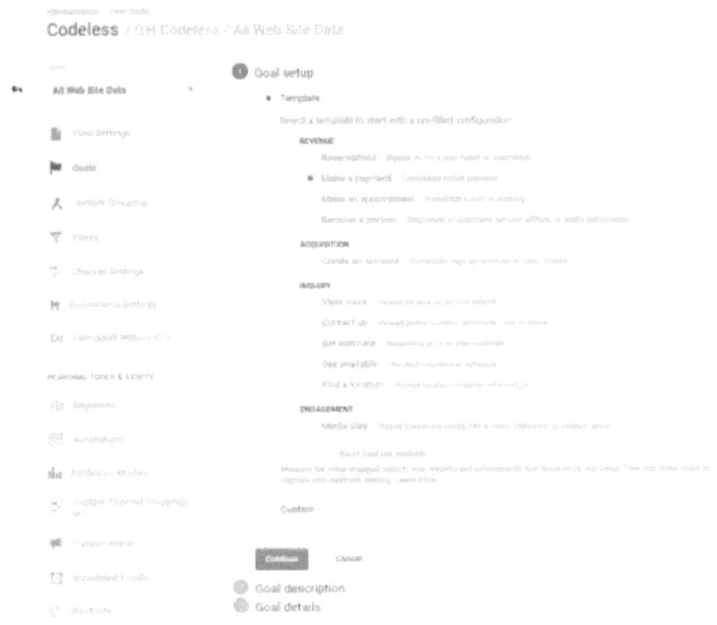

On the "Goal Setup" tab, click on the "Custom Radio" tab, scroll to the bottom and then click "Continue."

Goal Description

You will get a prompt to enter a name for your goal and select its type. Find any name that will make it easy to remember what you are tracking and click on "Destination" as the type. Click on the button titled "Continue."

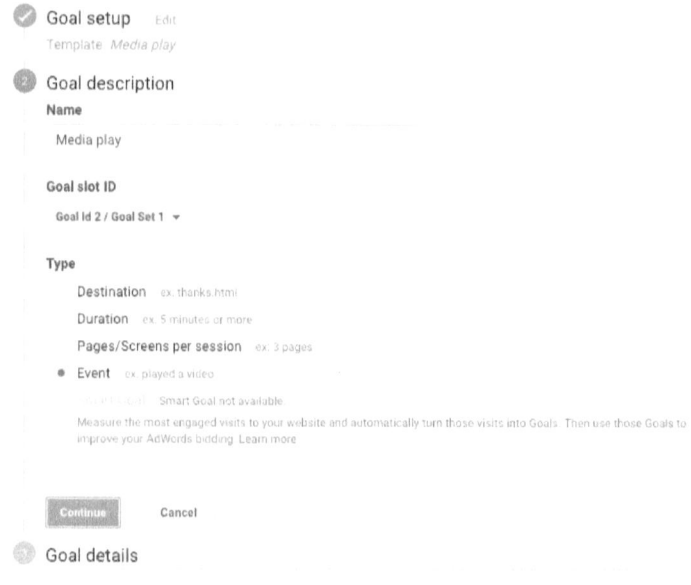

Fill in Goal Details

To make what conversion you are tracking more specific, you can add in your labels. The details start out broad and get more specific and include the category, the action, and the label.

Category – Usually includes general terms being tracked such as File, Video, or Outbound link.

Action – What the visitors are doing on the site, including options like Share, Play, Submit or Download.

Label – Smaller details you need, such as specific poll answers or colors of the items.

You should then select "Yes" to ensure that Event Values are transferred to Goal Values too. This will ensure that you can go back to the information and see the marketing campaigns, medium/source or channel that generated the visitor action.

With the goal details set up, you can create a goal for the macro conversion and then head back to the beginning and click "Acquisition." Enter a destination goal as the goal type and then drop in the URL for the confirmation or the "Thank You" page that someone lands on after they submit their information.

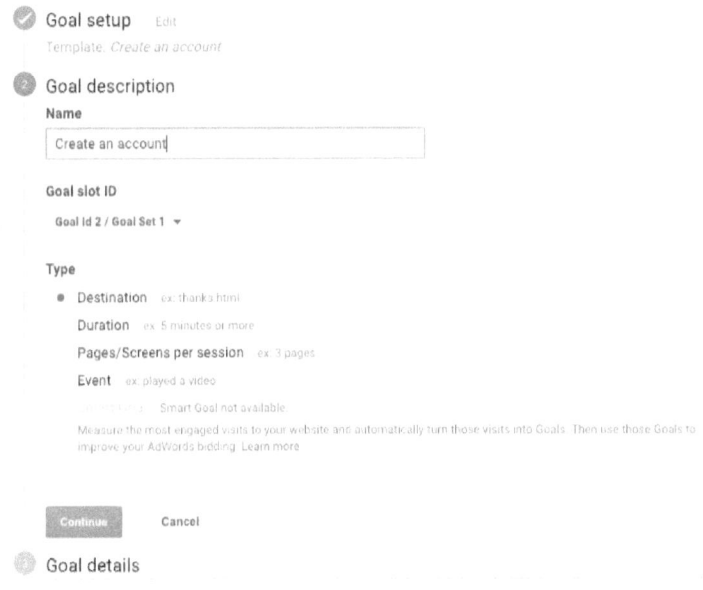

To Customize the Last Step

Enter the URL path for your confirmation page without the root domain. As such "https://example.com/thanks" should be simply: "/thanks":

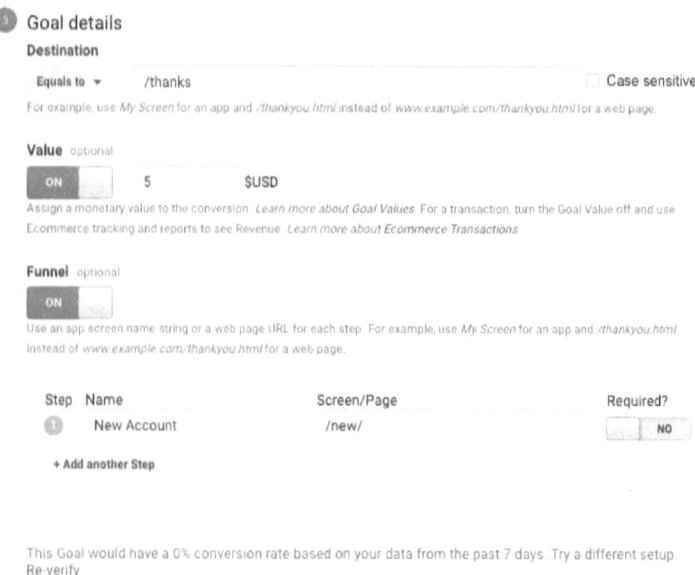

Now hit "Save" and you are done.

Start Recording

Once you have set up your goals, Google Analytics will start recording data.

View Your Data

Once you have your goals set up, begin by going to the main reporting tab of Google Analytics and click Conversions > Goals > Overview.

- ▼ ⚑ Conversions
  - ▼ Goals
    - Overview
    - Goal URLs
    - Reverse Goal Path
    - Funnel Visualization
    - Goal Flow
  - ▶ Ecommerce
  - ▶ Multi-Channel Funnels

HOW TO SET UP GOOGLE ANALYTICS ECOMMERCE TRACKING

If you are a seller of digital or physical products, you will need to track them using custom codes embedded in the shopping cart. With such tracking, you will be able to get important information such as:

1. Which pages are getting the most conversions?

2. What products are the most valuable?

3. How are people arriving at your important pages?

This information will make it possible to determine the most effective pages of your website so that you can optimize your sales funnels.

For instance, you could discover that one page is getting a good 20 percent conversion rate as compared to another that is only getting 5 percent. This may drive the decision to either tweak the poorly performing page or to spend less on that page while doubling down on the better performing landing page.

To get the important data from Analytics you will need to enable ecommerce reporting by switching on the Ecommerce set up on the Main Website Profile Information.

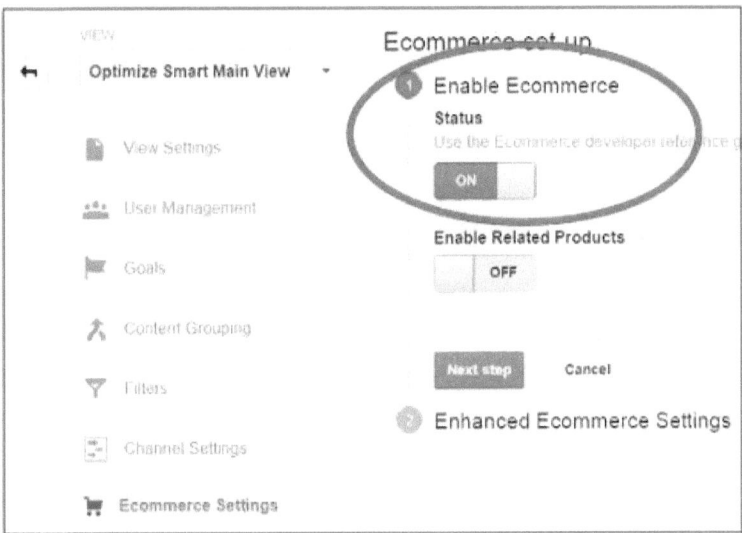

You will have to add a customized tracking code to the shopping cart system. This will collect data on how and when purchases occur. How to implement this will depend on the shopping cart and hosting provider. It can often be done through hand-coded HTML, a separate module on the CMS or through server-side inclusion.

Integrate Analytics with Google Ads

Integrating AdWords with Google Analytics can provide some important information on the effectiveness of your PPC campaigns. It also gives you critical information like what visitors do when they are on the website and what keywords convert better, amongst others.

This is a simple integration. All you need to have is an AdWords account and a Google Analytics account, both with the same email address. Log into your AdWords account and from the Reporting tab select "Google Analytics" and then select the account you need to integrate from the list.

Integrated Analytics, Step by Step

Ensure that you have associated a Google Analytics account with your website, and that you have the admin rights to the account you intend to integrate. Log in to the Google AdWords account and click on the tab "Tools and Analysis" and select "Google Analytics" from the menu. Click on the "Admin" tab.

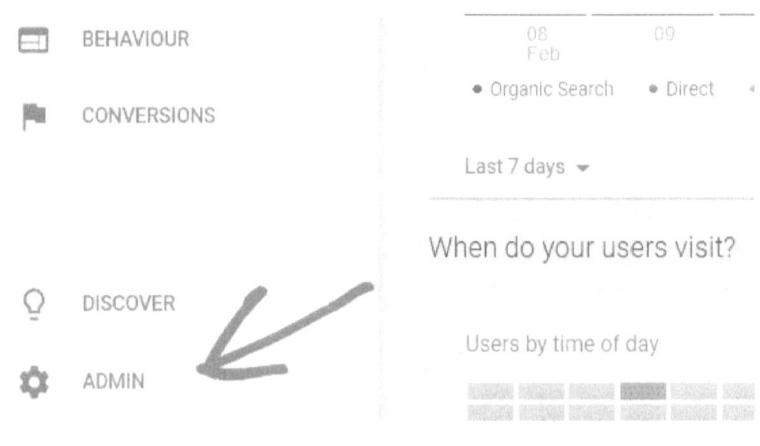

Click on the domain you intend to integrate with Analytics.

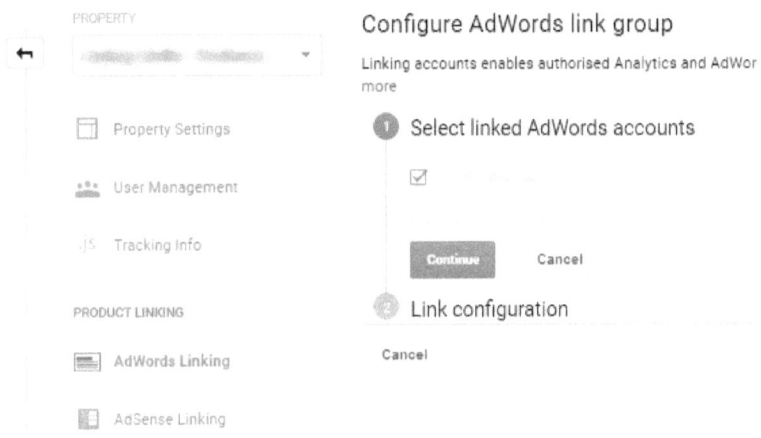

You can then link Google Analytics to the Google AdWords account. It is always recommended to let Google auto-tag your links.

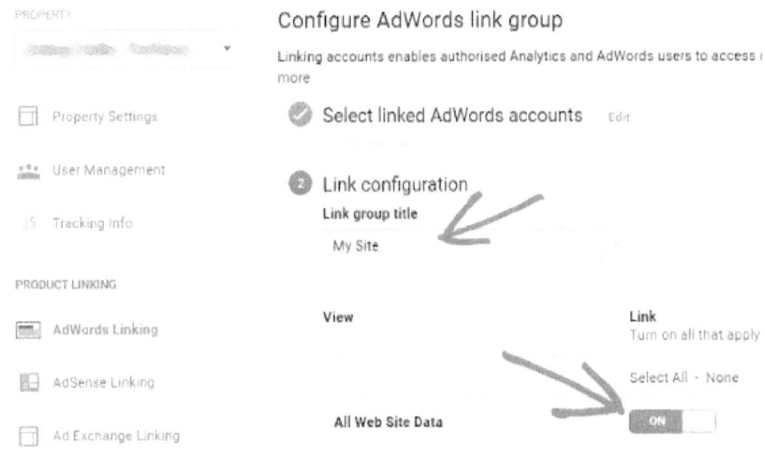

Once that is done, you can activate Google Analytics integration with the Google Ads account.

To do so, go to the ad group or campaign and/or keyword tab on the Google AdWords account, then click the "Settings" button. This will make it possible to select all the metrics you want to analyze. On the list of properties, click on the one you want to link and follow the process above to integrate Analytics and AdSense accounts.

CREATE YOUR SEO DASHBOARDS

There is a wealth of information in analytics to uncover if you know where to look. Google Analytics presents information in an easily digestible format via the dashboard interface. The Google Analytics dashboard is comprised of several widgets that compile the individual reports into one view that you can easily share, access or print. With a dashboard, you can reduce the time spent on analyzing metrics. This will free up your time so that you can focus on creating more content or optimizing content.

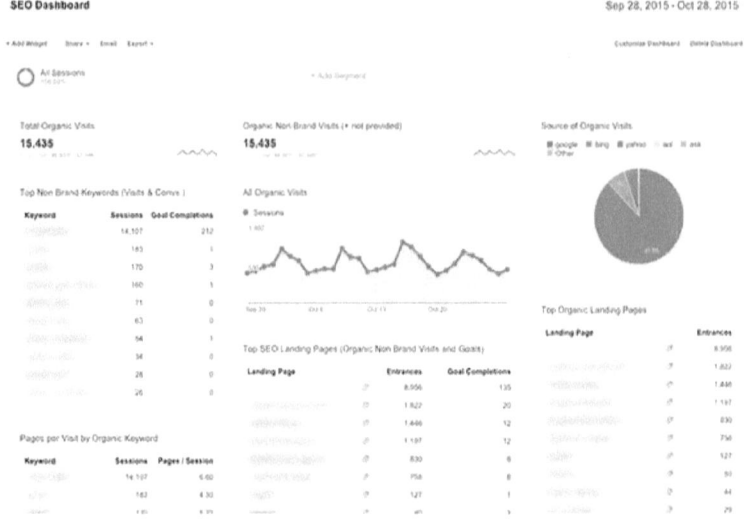

Some examples of dashboards that you can create include:

- Unique visitors
- Unique visitors from SEO, social media
- How people find your website: organic, referral, direct
- Top keywords
- Top viewed pages
- Social networks sending the most traffic
- Referral websites

Google Analytics also allows you to download dashboards by other users and integrate them into your own analytics account. Some recommended dashboards you can download are:

- Search Console Dashboard
- Content Consumption by Traffic Source Dashboard

- SEO Dashboard - Finding Top Content and Keywords

Ideally, you want to be able to track your content and have certain goals set up. Some of the metrics I would pay attention to are:

Pageviews – Are certain articles producing more visits than others? Which topics are they are? Why was that article so popular?

Bounce rate – This can be a deceiving metric. In most cases, visitors will hopefully find the information they seek in your content. If they see one page only and don't explore the site, it could be an issue. What can we do to improve the number of pages people read?

Time on page – If the bounce rate is high but time on page is more than 1 minute that's a good sign. It means people are engaged with your content (videos help). Engagement is a sign to Google that searchers find value in your content.

PRO TIP: If you noticed even as you're creating continuous content that traffic remains the same or decreases – you could have a serious issue that needs to be identified, as creating more content will not fix the problem. This could most likely be a technical issue.

MONITORING KEYWORDS

While you can get some keyword data from search console, it isn't always accurate and you only receive a fraction of the keywords your site ranks for. If you want to be able to track the phrases you are trying to rank for by using third party tracking tools.

I use SEMrush to track my rankings. However, it is a paid tool. I get a lot of additional features such as keyword research, competitive analysis, and many other important features. However, you could use any of the following tracking tools.

- Moz
- Hoth
- SEMrush
- SE Ranking

As you create content you want to add those questions and phrases to your ranking report. As search console starts to populate keywords for your content you will want to add those to your ranking software as well. Many of the one, two and even three keyword phrases may be too competitive to rank for out of the gate – it is still to keep an eye on them, especially if they are within the first 20 positions of Google (first two pages).

Tweaking and Optimizing Content

What happens after you've written content? How long should you wait to make changes?

If you've been able to write 5 articles a month or more, after about 8 months or so you should start seeing an increase in traffic. If you have a ranking tool tracking your phrases and questions, take a look and see where the content is ranking. Are the rankings bouncing around? If so, leave that phrase/question alone and move on to one that seems to have been flat for a while.

This can also be applied to content that's been on your site for some time. Here is how I look at it. When new content gets picked up by Google, it typically starts to bounce around. You can see the history of your key phrase ranking over time.

Below is a screenshot from SEMrush on a key phrase that has seen a lot of fluctuation in rankings. Now, 95 percent of your keywords will move around. Very few will stay consistent however, this kind of bouncing around is Google trying to figure out where your current content belongs.

Here is an example of a key phrase that has stayed consistent over the last few weeks. This is a page I would then try and make on-page adjustments to that post.

Let's use the example of "how to buy the perfect motorcycle helmet." If you were ranking on page two for the title of this article, I would add a line towards the end of the article. Something to the effect of; "Hopefully, this guide has taught you how to buy the perfect motorcycle helmet," In many cases, this is all that is needed to rank for that question – providing the content is informative and more than 1,000 words.

However, if your content is not ranking on the first two pages of Google and/or your site is new – you need to give the content more time. Also, if you don't have at least 60 pieces of content on your site don't pay too much attention to the rankings, as you'll need more content for Google to pay attention to it. How long will it take for Google to start ranking content? If you can consistently write content as described in this book you can expect to see an uptick in traffic in about 6 – 10 months.

PRO TIP: I've noticed that updated content works great. Updating older content once or twice a year helps keep it fresh and relevant in the eyes of Google. If you're monitoring all of the content you are creating, you should be touching up and revising the content at least that much. Some website owners remove the timestamp from their blog posts in order to confuse Google as to when the content was created. However, I find that if you update the date stamp at the time you update the content it seems to improve rankings.

WHY TRADITIONAL LINK BUILDING ISN'T ALWAYS NECESSARY

As someone who has been a digital marketing professional since 2004, I've always stressed the importance of link building. It is an unfortunate evil when it comes to ranking in Google. However, there is a way to do it that minimizes the negative impact link building could have on your site.

What You Need to Build Links Naturally

- Content is king here. Your content needs to be well written, informative and lengthy. Grammatical errors, misspellings, and poor content structure will impact the quality of your content.

- The amount of content you create is also important. If you can produce 60+ pieces of unique content in the first year to create a solid foundation.

- You need to become an expert in the field you're writing about. Write an "about us" page that talks about your experience in your industry.

- The next step is to work on using social media to help your content gain exposure and to gain natural incoming links. Sharing on social media is expected by Google and helps you to drive traffic and hopefully some fresh incoming links. There are several ways to build links that you can do yourself and will not look suspicious to Google.

  - Turn your content into a YouTube video. YouTube is the 2nd largest search engine and creating a video is easy. Send a link from your channel page back to your website. Also, include a link from every video to its respective blog post.

  - Use a summary of your article and turn it into a podcast. You can use a service such as Anchor. You can create a podcast in 5 minutes using just your phone and your content will be pushed to places such as iTunes, Spotify, Stitcher, and many other platforms. Anchor will also provide your podcast with a dedicated page on their domain that will link back to your website.

  - Turn your content into an infographic and share it on image platforms like Flickr.

  - Create a PDF or presentation and place it on the side such as SlideShare.

- Share your content on social media channels such as Twitter, LinkedIn, and other relevant social media channels.

You can find services on sites such as Fiverr that can help you create and share some of these multimedia files above for a reasonable cost.

Help Reporters Out and Gain a Link

There is a free service that is created for journalists who are seeking help from experts to aid them in a story they are writing. The name of this service is Help A Reporter Out. HARO has more than 800,000 journalists and writers who use their service. When you sign up for this free service, you can choose which category you want to receive notifications on. You can choose only the categories you are interested in or all of them.

You will receive daily emails with a summary of what each potential writer needs. If your expertise fits the request, you can reply with your answer as well as your bio and headshot (if requested). If your quote is used, you will receive a link back to your website.

I recommend creating a canned response so that you can easily copy and paste with your bio, link to your site, and your headshot. Once the digest email gets sent out to all the list recipients, journalists get flooded with emails. The key to getting cited on these websites is to be both informative and swift in your responses.

While this may be considered "link building," it's one of the more natural ways of doing so. You aren't paying to be listed on these sites.

Content That Speaks for Itself

A great way to generate content and even more backlinks to your content is to interview others in your industry. It could be a one-on-one or you could ask several experts and compile their answers into a post. In many cases, the experts themselves will link and share the content which will give the content a boost. Also, posts with statistics get shared and quoted quite often. What factual data can you collect and compile that others will find useful?

Are all of these above items enough to launch your site into higher rankings? Yes, and no. Links from these social channels are useful to give your content a push and hopefully, you can drive traffic from these channels.

However, by going after a longer key phrase and answering questions, you'll be able to rank without a lot of backlinks. In many cases, this kind of content gets naturally linked. Many times, forums rank for this type for content but in many cases, the questions are never definitively answered.

Your blog post will more than likely be cited as a source on personal blogs and forums. This is the best way to gain links as the content you likely will be placed on will be highly relevant. This is why being informative and detailed is the key to successful SEO, not keyword density. This is why articles over 1,000 words do well; thought-out content naturally contains a lot of text.

PRO TIP: When creating videos and presentations for use on different platforms, the summaries and titles should be unique to maximize the SEO and keywords of the content could potentially rank for by leveraging the domain authority of other sites.

THE RIGHT WAY TO STRUCTURE YOUR BLOG

After working on thousands of websites over the course of 16 years, I've seen one important element that can bring all of your content creation efforts to a halt. When it comes to writing blog posts, especially on WordPress, there is a flaw in how content is categorized. In WordPress, you have tags and categories.

Tags change the URL of a blog post and create a new unique URL for each tag you place within an article. This creates duplicate content, causing confusion within Google and problematic issues to your site's ability to rank content over time. I recommend using categories but instead.

Categories *do not change* the URL structure and you can tag articles into multiple categories. However, there are two major factors you must do to maximize your SEO potential.

1. Categories need to be located in either the main navigation page or as links in a side column. It should be located on every page of the blog for easy access.

2. You must use only summaries or the first few sentences of your blog post on category pages (you can use the "read more" function on WordPress). This prevents the full article from being shown on category pages which can cause duplicate content issues.

Google uses your site navigation (main navigation, sub-navigation and/or breadcrumbs) to understand the importance of the content within the rest of the site. Users should never need to hit that back button to find content. If a visitor needs to hit the back button to navigate the site, it lowers the "value" of the content.

Orphaned pages, or pages that are only found from one link on a website, typically do not rank well, as they are "orphaned" from the rest of the site's navigation. Keeping this simple rule in mind when designing a site will help keep pages indexed within Google.

Why Not Just "No, Index" Tagged URLs?

When you "no, index" a URL you are telling the search engines that they should not include a particular page within search results. You could use this as an option, but if you are using tags as a way for search engines to discover your content, they won't be able to index your content as the "no, index" tag will block most if not all of your content. This is why categories work better.

How to Get More Out of The Content You Create

1. You're spending a lot of time and money creating awesome content, but is posting it on your site all you can do with it? Of course not!

2. You can use it in your newsletter to remind subscribers that new content has been added to your site.

3. You can turn some of those articles into a video series that you can place on YouTube.

4. Turn the content into a whitepaper and have new visitors provide their name and email to download a copy of it.

5. Take your articles and build an eBook. Use it for lead generation or sell it.

Use affiliate links within your content to generate additional revenue. I would avoid linking to direct competition or linking too much inside your content. Too many links from different affiliate programs makes it harder to cash out, as revenue may be split by referencing too many programs.

It's important to not lose sight of the goal of the content you are creating. The goal is not just to drive organic traffic, but to also build brand recognition and, ultimately, sales. However, if you litter your content with tons of affiliate links, you will be trading big business in actual customers for pennies made from affiliate offers.

Existing Content Optimization

If your site has more than 40 pieces of content and has been around for more than a year, it may be time to review your content. This book has outlined everything you need to create and research content. Apply what you've learned to your existing content.

- Is the site navigation set up properly?
- How informative is the existing content?
- Are you targeting the right keywords and questions?
- Do you have your titles and meta descriptions optimized?
- Have you shared your content on social media and created other multimedia elements around the content?

Once you review the titles of your articles, you'll be surprised that they aren't optimized and are possible driving little traffic, most of which is irrelevant.

You should now have everything you need to start driving organic traffic to your website. The most difficult part of all of this is being consistent with your content writing. Plan out your content as far in advance as possible, using an editorial calendar. This will help you stay on track and reach your goal.

If you've purchased this book in print form, you are eligible to receive a free copy of the digital version. If you've purchased a digital copy of the book and would like to purchase a print copy, contact Joe at Joe@JoeBalestrino.com

www.ingramcontent.com/pod-product-compliance
Lightning Source LLC
Chambersburg PA
CBHW021420210526
45463CB00001B/459